START YOUR OWN BUSINESS

To see a complete list of Management Books 2000 titles,
visit our web-site at http://www.mb2000.com

START YOUR OWN BUSINESS

Linden Cole

2000

First published in 2000 by Management Books 2000 Ltd
Cowcombe House
Cowcombe Hill
Chalford
Gloucestershire GL6 8HP
Tel. 01285 760 722
Fax. 01285 760 708
E-mail: mb2000@compuserve.com

Printed and bound in Great Britain by Biddles, Guildford

British Library Cataloguing in Publication Data is available
ISBN 1-85252-333-6

Contents

Author's Note

This book is dedicated to you, members of the great working public who, for whatever reason, want to break free of the shackles of working for someone else. Whether it's because you want to do for yourself, or because you want to get rich, or even because you're fed up where you are, this book is for you.

In writing this book, I have anguished over what to, and what not to include. Should I talk about computers, or other fancy techniques and tools like websites and e-commerce? These matters are important, so have included them, but most important is to get going. I try to keep things simple and straightforward. If something is too complicated, then the chances are that it's not for now. What I want to ensure is that you start out the right way – get the basics right.

This book brings together a wealth of experience that is now yours to own and apply. It will not give you the answer to every question, but I hope it will make you want to ask more.

I would like to thank many colleagues and friends, clients and antagonists who have helped to form and focus my ideas … and my darling wife standing over me as I write this note. To them – the base of my thoughts from which my experience has grown – a debt of gratitude.

Read on, have fun and I hope that this book will help to make you a real success story. The hard work will, as always, be down to you; this book should help … more than a little! Good luck, if you've got this far, you deserve it.

And now ... it is up to you.

Linden Cole

1

Introduction

This book has been written just for you. You have the potential to stand out from the crowd and be a real success, and you stand able to take the rewards that success brings. It only remains for you to take that step, that leap into the future.

If you look around any city, town or village – everywhere that people live and work – you will find those who have taken control of their own destiny. For them, people just like you, self-employment or running their own business is just a way of life. The local shopkeeper, the decorator, taxi drivers, contract workers (and there are a lot of those), hairdressers, many publicans and the vast army of people doing jobs that we do not even see, these and many more are self-employed.

Some, though, are more successful than others. Some just seem to survive, just bumble along and use their business to maintain a good lifestyle, while others really make a success out of life. The secret lies not in what you do – it's all about how you do it.

How does this book aim to help you?

It gives some important clues on the attitudes and beliefs needed to be a success, and helps you to overcome natural inertia and to 'put your best foot forward'. It explains some of the fundamentals, so that you can start a business with your eyes open. You will find some of the basic rules and strategies you can use to win.

Obviously this book will not make you an expert, but at least you will be better equipped to start.

This book outlines the importance of business planning and goes some way towards explaining the logic and structure you should use. There are many agencies that publish items such as 'How to write a business plan'. I do not try to replicate these. My aim is to get to the ideas and thoughts that should be going through your mind. I aim to make your planning more effective and valuable.

It is one thing to start a business, quite another to make a success of it. This book goes into some essential, basic ideas about business control to ensure that you will be more likely to achieve or exceed your plans. It take the wraps off finance and looks at options open to those who want financial help, at whatever stage of their business. It also takes some of the mystique away from the bank manager, and I aim to help you get the most out of someone who really should be an ally (if you know how to treat him).

There is no real magic to selling and marketing. It is a numbers game and plain common sense – especially at the small business level. The more effort you put into selling, the more sales will come out. There are therefore strategies for beating recessions and tips on how to actually sell as opposed to taking orders. This book also takes a cheeky look behind the scenes at how you can consider pricing, how pricing communicates more than you image about you, your product or service!

Despite best intentions, with so much going on, all businesses take their eyes off the reasons they started – to make money. As a result, many firms are bobbing along only just breaking even – or worse. I give a dozen or so tips on how to look at your business and wring profit out of it, indeed in some cases make more profit from doing a lot less work. Keeping this in mind stops problems arising in the first instance.

Being your own boss really does work, despite the problems and the heartaches. At some time in the future, if the pundits have it right, most of us will start a business or simply call ourselves self-employed and fend for our own incomes. Job security is now a thing of the past. Working for yourself could well be the best thing that ever happened to you.

8

If it works for you, being your own boss is really great, it's fantastic and what is in this book will help you want to try, and then succeed. You will become proud of your achievements. You will want to do well and, most importantly, you will think differently. You will see the world from a different direction, and equally important, different skills and attitudes will be asked and expected of you.

But why, when I make it sound easy, do not more people do it, and when they do, some seem to fall by the wayside. You need to adopt the right approach and stick to it. A good business person is just someone who keeps to the basics more than somebody else does.

No book can do it all for you, and you will need an idea of what you want to do. What this book aims to do, in a few words, is try to give you a good grounding in the basics of business sense so that, with application on your part, your business will be a success.

2

Be a Winner

Winning depends upon your attitude and outlook. Invariably it comes because you want to win and are prepared to do what it takes. As long as you have drive and commitment, you can achieve whatever you set out to do. Really!

How do you decide if you've got the right attitude? There is no perfect combination, and you must do and be what is right for you. The following are some useful pointers as to the sort of outlook that will make life easier, make winning in business more certain.

Life, a positive approach

Keep a positive outlook – look on the bright side of life. Adopt a 'can do' attitude. There is no such word as can't.

Nobody wants to hear about your problems, not even the Samaritans. On the other hand, everyone wants to know how you are going to overcome those problems or, better still, that you have no problems at all. Even those willing to help in hours of need are trying to help you get rid of problems. Many people will help you succeed, but you must be positive. Be ahead of the game, help yourself as well as looking for help from others. A sure sign of maturity is being able to ask for help, and accept it. But maturity is also helping yourself by not focusing on problems.

It is imperative to speak positively. This helps you to build your self-confidence … and confidence in others. If you speak with a positive voice, you will create an atmosphere to match. If you use negative words, then you commit yourself to a negative attitude and 'failure' becomes the norm – success then becomes so much more difficult to achieve. Never talk yourself down – always up.

So many people wait for opportunity to knock on their door and fail to see it at the window. Too many people wait for opportunity to come to them rather than go looking for it. If you have trouble seeing opportunity, then you are not looking in the right area, or you have not been looking the right way, or you've been looking at it for so long you just cannot see it. Look again. Look for opportunity – then, when it comes, you will see it. Opportunity is there for us all. There's bags of it about.

Be enthusiastic.

Pessimists often accuse me of being naive, but without enthusiasm, you are closed to ideas – the life-blood of the future. The very essence of business is enthusiasm. Enthusiasm is a vital ingredient, and will see you over many difficult times.

- Enthusiasm is contagious and it grows in importance as time goes on.
- Speaking to customers, talking to bank managers, getting staff to go that extra step – where would you be if you were not positive and enthusiastic?
- Who will be enthusiastic about your efforts if not you!
- Be enthusiastic about yourself, your business, your product, your service and the value that you give to clients.
- Without this enthusiasm for what you do, who is going to enthusiastic enough to buy from you?

In staff, enthusiasm is an underrated issue. Most companies look for and promote staff who are technically skilled, yet when people are sacked, in most cases it is because of poor attitude and lack of motivation. In my mind, enthusiasm should prove to be the main criterion when employing or promoting people. There are some very critical lessons for what is important in employees … and of course, in yourself.

11

Never fear failure

In business you must do well. This brings with it the possible stigma of potential failure felt at the very core of why most people never try do anything for themselves. It is a part of the British culture – those who don't succeed are branded as failures. So, out of fear of being so branded, most people don't even try, or don't try as hard as they should (which conversely make success harder to achieve). I do not say this to put you off trying, but to make you more determined to succeed, more determined to do what is necessary – not just enough to get by.

Success is a state of mind, and often it is those people who never try who are first to brand non-success as failure. Here is a simple exercise for you – try making two lists.

☞ The first list is quite easy when you settle down to it. List all the things you have done when you have had success. Friendships, clubs, learning to swim or ride a bike, driving, a family, exams, promotions, music, owning a home, past business efforts, getting a job – it doesn't matter, they are all successes. If you need more paper, fine, get more. You can probably fill several A4 sheets without much effort. Just be positive.

☞ Now think of all those things that have not worked out as planned, but where you have not learned or not gained experience. I doubt if there is one single entry. Okay, maybe a few, but certainly not many. Even if in the past you have tried and failed, then you should have learned from the experience – so that cannot be seen as a failure. At worst this could be a costly lesson. At least you can now start to look at life positively.

By comparing the lists, you should start to realise that success and failure are personal views and, if we stay positive, there is no such thing as failure. You are not a failure! You never were. Remember that success is a state of mind. You succeed. You may not succeed as well as you'd hoped, but you do succeed.

If at first you don't succeed, try, try again

We all know it and agree with the idea, then forget about it. The Americans have a more open view of the world – they see trying and learning from mistakes as an essential part of life. In many parts of the world, to have tried and failed is seen as an essential part of learning about business. You won't make the same mistakes twice.

Success is very important to us all. It comes in various forms and guises. It is something often elusive until, when you start to recognise it, it becomes an old and trusted friend. Once you recognise success, you find it following you about everywhere.

Positive Expectations – picture the future

People who succeed do so because they know where they are going and know how they are going to get there. It is all down to having a vision of what you want the world to look like for you and yours into the future. If you don't know where you are going, then you are going nowhere!

We become what we think about, what we aim towards, what we desire, that to which we aspire. Understand what you want, understand the effort needed and the rewards will surely come. It will have a price. Understanding and effort are the route to success. The following is a simplistic yet fundamental way of keeping ahead. Understand what's needed, make the effort needed and the results should come.

Understanding x Effort = Result

How many times have you heard people say that something is impossible, cannot be done. And yet people do achieve just what others believe impossible. It is the basic difference between those who do and those who don't – a belief that something can be done.

The message from the Bible is that faith conquers all. This is really true. It is a state of mind, an attitude. Whether in economic terms or

13

performance of your business, or goals that you set for yourself or your staff, you must believe that you can achieve them. The first premise of leadership is that you have faith in what you are doing, where you are going.

You get what you expect in life – successful people expect success. If you expect your business to do well, then the chances are it will. If you expect difficulties then those difficulties will be there, just as you foresaw. If you expect to lose, you will. Worse, if you just do not expect to win, your business will amble along until problems arise, by which time you have lost positive impetus and your business will never reach it's potential.

A damning statistic I heard somewhere is that we can expect 30% of all companies to close within the next 3 years.

Do not let it be yours.

Live for now

Unhappiness is allowing your life to be governed by what may happen – even though it's in your own hands to determine what will be. There is seldom a better time than now to do what you want. The clock never stops, tomorrow never arrives, so there is no time like the present. Don't put off 'til tomorrow what you can do today.

Mid-life crises are well known, and they come when we realise that life won't go on forever. For men, these traditional times are the mid-40s, for women probably in their late 30s. It is then that we realise it is not the length but the quality of life that counts. So you have to ask the question "Am I wasting time?" Waste money and you've only wasted money, waste time and it cannot be replaced. If you've wanted to try, but haven't yet, time is running out.

The same holds true for action. If you are going to do something, unless there is an exceptionally good reason not to, do it now! There is never a better time than the present. That way, things will not be put off, and a stitch in time does save nine!

Who is really important?

There is the story I heard once about the smiling maiden. A young girl was out walking one day when she saw a butterfly

14

trapped in a spider's web. Freeing it, she found that the butterfly turned into a fairy, who offered the girl the secret of happiness as a reward. From that point on and all through her life she smiled and was known for always being happy, but never told anyone why.

Then, when an old lady, she was asked directly by a young man why she was always so happy. After much pleading she relented and told her story and what the fairy had said. "The fairy told me that no matter how rich or successful others are, they all need me. No matter what it is that I do, there is always purpose and value to everything I do, and I am everybody's equal."

So put what you are and what you want into the bigger picture. You are as good and as important as anyone else is, so:

- Stop being lazy, being afraid and being self-deprecating – these are blocks to potential.

- Remember you only use a fraction of your potential – you have the scope to be exceptional. Einstein is reputed only to have used around 10% of his potential.

- In all of this, do not forget to be kind to yourself and your family (or the chances are that business will have some costs you didn't expect).

- Too much freedom is restrictive – give your life some structure and value. Give yourself a framework to work within and you will find life more enjoyable.

- Life is based around people – relationships matter – staff, customers and family, as well as the general society in which you live.

Can you do it?

Of course you can – if you go about it the right way and get all the help you need. The things that are most likely to stop you are things you imagine as problems – things that really do not exist.

There is not really a particular type of person who, in my eyes, is the right or the wrong 'stuff' for starting a business. What is critical is to know yourself and to understand what you are good at. You must know your strengths and weaknesses and act accordingly. Play to your strengths and overcome your weaknesses. Do not allow problems to develop, and always remember that strength taken to its extreme under different circumstances, can be a weakness.

Business becomes an extension of you, of your personality. It takes on your values, good or bad, and reflects you as an individual. There are those who say that being in business takes away your human instinct. I disagree. I would say that business lays bare those parts of you which otherwise get fudged.

When it's down to the basics – and it soon gets down to basics – the gloves come off and the person you really are stands there in all of your glory. You will live by your qualities and fall by your weaknesses.

As we move into the future, so the nature of business will shift. Success will be judged on how well you relate to people, and how well you delight your customers (customer satisfaction is becoming the norm). There is an old proverb – 'What you give is what you get'. It is true.

You get back what you put in. My mother used to call it balance, and she was right. In the long run, you receive in equal measure to what you give. If you want a lot, then you have to learn to give a lot. If you want people to respect you, you must respect others. If you expect customers to stay loyal, then you must make them WANT to stay loyal – there are many who will try very hard to take your customers away.

Nowadays we have choice.

Many people in business, especially in the 'passing trades' end of the market, call their customers 'punters'. What a dreadful way to address the person who after all will pay the wages. 'Punters' sums up all the feelings of low value you have for those upon whom you depend. 'Punters' will end up being someone else's value customers. Value *your* customers..

Risk ... the downside

It would be folly to say that there are no risks, that it is all plain sailing. There are two real sorts of risk:

- **financial** – it is most likely that you have your money and future tied up in your business

- **emotional** – when things do not go well.

This book will give you many ideas for reducing risk, but the dangers will never go away.

Financial risk

The financial risk is fairly obvious, and living with that risk is something you will learn to do. It is a fact of life – the risk is managed and it is lived with. That so many people are in business shows that the risk can be overcome, but that businesses go under shows it is always there. You can and should protect yourself against the risks. The reassuring thing is that risk can be managed, if not largely removed. A subtle way I heard of describing risk is that it is like something on your shoe that the dog left on the footpath. Being prepared for problems and knowing how to get out of trouble is like having a tissue to hand. Fortunately, there are many people around to help if you just ask!

Business life is all about the continual dealing with risk and the consequences of making the wrong decision. Risk comes in many forms. If you don't at least break even, you will have to stand the loss. If the business can't pay the bills or the wages, then you will have to find the money yourself or borrow from the banks – and that is becoming less easy unless you do it the right way. Few people really realise when they start their own businesses that if they fail, they could literally lose everything. Life is littered with those who have tried, failed and have lived to regret it. But with the risk goes the reward, the rewards come to those who take a risk. Fortunately there are many more successes than 'business failures'. And if your first business doesn't work – remember you can try again!

17

Emotional risk

Risk is not only financial, it is emotional. Everyone in business cannot help but let the good bits and bad bits of business life rub off. The good times are really good. The bad bits are less so. You get very used to these excesses, they become normal and without them life becomes a touch boring.

Are you good enough?

Most people initially do not see themselves as able to make the grade, in being able to succeed as controller of their own business. Rubbish! To set out in business is an incredible learning experience and great fun – never an easy ride, but great fun. It helps to have someone with whom you can talk things over. This becomes far more beneficial if you can talk over a decision you are about to make.

Being in business can also be a lonely place, and if you can find a friend with whom you can talk, then do so. Between partners, even man and wife, the art of talking becomes forgotten and the loneliness can become invasive. Responsibility is a heavy burden when carried all the time, and to share the load if only for a while makes it much easier to bear.

Perhaps it is the pressures you face, the many hats you must wear, which make it so difficult for your staff, however diligent, to understand their boss. It is only the unusually sensitive employee that understands you. One more problem, one more pressure. Pressure will be there and will get to you as surely as it gets to everyone at some time.

Are you optimistic? Even if this is tinged with a degree of realism, you will need lots of optimism to take you through what will include some hard times and some sacrifice on the way to the good times. Optimism can be very advantageous but you must not let it overcome common sense and lead you to do foolish things.

If you have staff, you will recognise the need to stay optimistic even through bad times. If you are worried, you can bet that everyone sees your fears – and they start worrying themselves. You soon learn that even if you do not feel too optimistic, then you must look all smiles. And when you smile, that conveys all sorts of good vibrations that find their way back to you in strange ways. If you smile, even in bad times, things do not look quite so bad. Even the worst of problems can be lived through. It's hardest for families where communication breaks down, where men and women deal with stress in differing ways, and where you feel the effect of their problems.

You will never understand your potential until you have made the move. Some people have never worked for anybody else and feel the same fears in reverse. The only way to find out is to try, then to look back and assess yourself with the benefit of hindsight. You will be amazed how far you have come in a short time, how much you have grown as a person, how much you have changed.

Acknowledge success!

But what is 'success'? Well, that is going to vary according to what it is you are going to do, and so will not be the same for everybody. There are however a few thoughts to bear in mind which will certainly impact the way others view you.

- ☑ Accept all compliments with at least a simple 'thank you'.
- ☑ Dress and look the part – but above all be clean and tidy irrespective of the work you do – even landscape gardeners are expected to be clean when not digging.
- ☑ Enjoy volunteering your name first – volunteer and be visible.
- ☑ Walk erect – look forward, be positive and stride quickly.
- ☑ Accept yourself, your strengths and foibles, and enjoy yourself.
- ☑ Set internal standards and aim to beat them.
- ☑ Have a self-development plan – how will you personally grow?
- ☑ Stay positive.
- ☑ Have a deep sense of your own worth.
- ☑ Don't just talk about doing it – DO IT.

So, to conclude, have you got what it takes to be a winner? The answer must be a positive 'yes!' Do you want to be a winner in business? That is for you to decide. But if you do, then there should be little to stop you .... that is, except yourself!

3

Action Speaks Louder Than Words

In business, there are too many people who keep getting ready ... just to get ready. They never seem to actually do anything. They just talk about it. But to succeed, you've actually got to get out there and DO.

The 7 steps

There are basically seven steps to follow to start DOING rather than talking about it. There is a premise behind this. There is never enough information. So accept that there will never be a perfect time. There is no time like the present.

The 7 steps are:

1. *Identify what it is you want to do.* There are far too many people who just do things almost without reason. First decide what business you are going to be in, what service you will offer, or what you are going to do.

2. *Clarify any deadlines*, and if they are too far away, break them down into manageable chunks so that the task is not too large to be tackled.

3. *List the obstacles* that stand in your way – often not as many in reality as you first think.

4. **Decide the resources** you need – or have available to you.

5. **Plan the route** you want to take – the actual things you will do, and when you will do them.

6. **Understand what benefits are expected** – to keep you motivated when you are 'doing'.

7. Finally, **just do it**, don't worry, don't fret, just do something.

> **'A journey of a 1000 miles starts with a single step.'**

The problem is the first step. When you are under way, it seems so much easier, and those imagined problems shrink. Action is the best remedy for worry.

Barriers, what barriers?

There are few barriers that cannot be overcome. Of these, the majority are in the mind and are but a few.

Stepping into the unknown always induces fear. You fear the loss of a secure income, which your family depends on after all. You are seldom the master or mistress of your own destiny whilst you work for another. There is less security in employment nowadays, and change is becoming the norm. Self-employment though is quite the reverse. The only person who determines your fate is ... YOU.

Procrastination – something we will discuss in greater detail later – is a killer of good intentions. From finding excuses to reasons why not to move, from being too busy to get things done to waiting for the perfect time – these are all so-claimed reasons why action should be delayed. They are not reasons at all, they are excuses – so admit it!

Friends are a major barrier to progress in many cases. Friends want to maintain the status quo, and the more they like you, the less they want you to move on. Never ask the advice of a friend, a colleague once advised me, and he was right. Friends are over-cautious, they want the best for you ... but best in their eyes. It is a courageous friend who selflessly advises you to do something that they couldn't or wouldn't do. Of course, not everyone is the same, so it isn't a hard and fast rule, but beware.

There are many other barriers that you will imagine in your way. Barriers are there to break through! Go under, over, round or through them. Better still, ignore or just overcome the issue. Seek out others like yourself – even if you don't know them at present. Plan and navigate your route, believe in your goals and GO FOR THEM.

Tips for getting things done.

There are many tips for being an achiever, and many books written around the subject. Enough then for me to give a few vital ones – which are after all just application of common sense. These are:

☑ Break your business plan down into things you can manage and achieve – from a 5-year plan to a 1-year program, then to a 6-month campaign, monthly goals and weekly lists.

☑ Break the day down into time slots and set aside definite slots to do specific things (not all day, just set aside a couple of slots you are in total control of).

☑ Have 'to do lists' so that you keep a record of what you are intending to do, and when. You can cross them off the list when they are done.

☑ Set priorities – and deal with high priority issues before they become urgent.

☑ Deal with problems a day at a time – do not worry about things that are not due yet else these worries (which may not happen) will stop you doing what you need today.

Key words in business

There are several key words in business which must never be forgotten – which are the key to succeeding. These key words are all positive and must precede all statements. They include:

Opportunity, succeed, shall, now, achieve, want to, can do, will do, and of course ... do!

People and decisions share one strength – they are both emotional and therefore can be managed. Embrace changes, welcome them, and action becomes so much more natural. Put positive emotion on your side!

Procrastination

This is defined in my dictionary as *'to put off (an action) until later, delay, postpone until tomorrow'*. It is the enemy of all action, a killer of business, yet so natural to people generally – thriving on and encouraging comfort. Procrastination is destructive, and only gives a temporary release from problems. When you procrastinate, the problem does not go away, it simply gets bigger in your mind – thus making it harder to face when tomorrow comes.

Some signs of procrastination:

- ☒ You plan ... but never do.
- ☒ You avoid difficult work – just do easy jobs.
- ☒ You put off menial or routine tasks.
- ☒ You stick with a job that is too small for you.
- ☒ You are often sick.
- ☒ You avoid confrontation ... except with family, who receive all your frustration.
- ☒ You blame outside circumstances beyond your control – it's not your fault.
- ☒ You give negative criticism.
- ☒ You refuse other's help ... Why?
- ☒ You use the phrase – 'It's boring!'

23

There are five key things to remember to overcome what is quite a natural urge (at the moment) to put things off. These are:

☑ Just get started – just do a little.

☑ Do not be afraid – the fear is often imaginary.

☑ Don't put off what appears at first to be unpleasant.

☑ Do it yourself – don't wait for others to make a start.

☑ Don't fear failure – relish trying.

Once you have spotted that you are like the majority of people and put off doing jobs where you are uncertain of how to proceed, or where you just don't fancy doing them, how do you move forward?

There are several tips for procrastinators – and yes, believe me, they apply to everyone no matter how little confidence you may have:

☑ Do the first thing now, not tomorrow – NOW.

☑ Seek out the expertise – if need be, borrow a book or ask for help.

☑ Remember how good you actually are – and that you cannot be perfect at everything.

☑ Do the least pleasant things first – that way they're done.

☑ Visualise completion.

☑ Give it 100% of your effort for 10 minutes – that will not feel so bad.

☑ Give public commitment to achieving your tasks and that will make it harder to back down.

☑ Give yourself a reward for completion.

☑ Don't cheat even once – you will only kid yourself.

☑ If necessary, become an automaton – JUST DO IT.

Business is about action. Work smart certainly, but just get it done. Do not put it off. If it's easy, then do it the easy way – if it's hard, do it the hard way, but just do it.

Self-motivation

Self-motivation, getting yourself moving, is an important skill. It does not come naturally but is an essential ingredient for success. Having that spark of energy really does make a difference. Those with it succeed, those without do not. The following tips will help:

- Do not try to motivate yourself – or others – with fear (unless it is safety driven). This only makes things harder.

- Do things now – beginning is half done.

- Go looking for opportunity but do not try doing too many things at once – that way, you will finish nothing and will get little satisfaction from success.

- Focus on the target – keep your eye on the goal. A problem only exists in your mind because there are practical solutions to nearly everything – even lack of finance.

- Never compare yourself with others – just do your best. You never know their situation and remember that appearances can be deceptive.

- Give yourself (and recognise) some early and easy successes.

- Remember there are only a few basic human stories and problems – everything is just a variation on these so your situation is not unique, no matter how it may seem so at the moment.

- Break old habits such as always turning on the television when you walk into the room or get home. Stop inertia.

- Get noticed – tell people what you are doing.

Self-motivation is a key to success, it is about the desire and the willingness, and the persistence, to overcome problems.

Goals

Goals are a precursor to action. No goal, no target, no focus – then action is wasted and effort is easily diffused. A dream will stay a dream until you put some numbers around it, make it a goal, and go for it. Goals are important in a business context because they are actual, specific measures that allow you to see whether you have achieved what you said you would, and are thus the basis of control. Your financial statements in your business plan are just measures of what will happen if you do what you say or plan. Thus you can see by comparing plan to reality whether you are in fact doing as well as you said – or better.

Success is making a habit of doing things well – goals are important and comparing actual with plan is an important discipline to develop.

Remember – when achieving goals:

- replace 'can't' with 'can'
- replace 'try' with 'will'
- focus energy on the objective
- look for solutions, not more work.

Start from here.

There is no place or time like the present to start doing. Clean out your mental closets and accept today's reality. Become self-reliant. The clock stops for no man, so it is running as we speak. The time is now.

The world seems to stand aside for those who tread a definite path, for people like you who know where they are going. Perhaps because the rest of society is so wishy-washy, the person with direction and purpose is going cut a swathe.

Do not try to do everything

Take things one step at a time. It is impossible to go out for a meal and try everything on the menu. Pick the thing you want most, and come back another time to try other dishes you fancy.

Life is all about cause and effect – if you don't start then you cannot succeed. Worse, once you have thought of starting out for yourself and you fail to do so, then you will forever be wondering what would have happened if you had done. Better to regret doing something that didn't work as you expected, then move on, than to regret never doing it at all!

Remember that lack of action actually increases stress, increases fatigue, creates clutter in your life and makes doing things later much harder – by then, there are other things to do. It is surprising to me that the more you seem to do, the more it enables you to do things more easily. The more work you actually do, the more work you can do. You also develop the knack of working smarter rather than harder. Once you start, your productivity goes up immensely. There is never any time like the present.

Be Charismatic

Turn good ideas into practice, but remember that in business, as good as an idea is, it is people who count – customers, staff, friends, suppliers, bankers, the public (future customers) and so on. So, several tips on getting ahead with people:

- ☑ Project a charismatic and warm personality – be friendly and smile.

- ☑ First impressions count and you only get one chance to make a first impression – make sure yours is a good one.

- ☑ The least impressive person is one who tries to impress – be natural.

- ☑ The way to encourage interest from other people is to show interest in what they are doing.

- ☑ Try to look the part and live up to other people's expectations – but do not flaunt wealth because that creates a barrier where none is necessary.

☑ Introduce yourself positively and with warmth.

☑ The best way to let someone know you understand them is to listen actively. They will love it as interest shown in them and their problems. You will be their friend.

☑ Adopt an attitude that service is essential and that you will give it – even though they will end up paying for it.

☑ Make people glad they talked to you – the secret of communication.

☑ Smile – as often as you can.

Practice makes perfect

Action is all about doing, but doing does not guarantee getting it right, nor does it make it easy or natural. The one thing that really helps here is practice. Practice makes perfect, and helps iron out those niggly faults that make you ineffective. There are several benefits of practice.

● Practice conditions your mind to reinforce winning habits. This makes you believe what you say and makes you much more convincing (even though it may sound false to you!).

● We are what we do, see and think – we can therefore see things through our own eyes and not be a spectator whilst things are happening.

● Dwelling on desired outcomes reinforces the future, not mistakes of the past. You can observe that when a sportsperson misses a shot or performs badly – he or she visibly acts out what should have been done.

● In the longer term, your mind absorbs what you practice and makes it the natural, correct way of doing things, so that you find you become the skilled person you want to be.

Whether you say you can, or you say you can't, you are right. If you want to, then you can. Practice makes what you want easier, it helps you realise that you can win without the pain of failure in front of customers. It takes away the fear that has to be the enemy of potential. Courage is not absence of fear, it is control of fear. Practice makes that easier.

What is fear?

Perhaps the neatest definition of fear I have encountered was from a motivational course. False Expectancies Appear Real – FEAR. It is natural to worry. But these worries are often groundless.

Fear does stop a lot of people making decisions. "What if I'm wrong?" Do not worry, failure is seldom the result of one major event, although it can be the accumulation of lots of little events.

More likely though, failure will be the result of not doing something when you should, or leaving things so long that they are done shoddily (or not at all). It takes as much effort to do things later – probably more – and as much effort to do things shoddily. If you are worried about doing something, remember that action speaks louder than words – get help, try, and do your best (but do not necessarily try for perfection). Action is the way to defeat fear.

Your life is your responsibility, and your fate is in your own hands. Losers let things happen, winners drive the future. You may decide never to start a business. You may be forced to later. You may decide to strike out at the right time, but you must decide. If you just let the future happen, then it just will. If you are not a prime mover, you are not likely to be the major beneficiary.

You are the chief agent of your life and you must make the decisions between the options and alternatives you see before you. That requires self control and appropriate response to the future as you face it. You must be responsible for how the future unfolds. The only way for the future to be what you want, for you to get the things and the life you want is for you to go out there and ...

MAKE IT HAPPEN!

4

Some business ground rules

All businesses go through similar stages of development. There are, as I have said, some very basic ground rules that need to be observed as these stages are developed. It is important to get the basics 100% right, but unfortunately the majority of new businesses do not.

What do you intend doing? Perhaps the hardest thing to do is come up with an idea. What business should you have, and why will yours succeed?

This is the age of competition, quality and service. You must provide what the customer wants. You must stand out from the norm where it matters to the customer. You must be special – not just in the product or the service you offer, but also in the back-up you provide, the support you give, the priority you give to customers' specific needs and your speed of response. You need to set yourself apart from the rest of the field. Aim for excellence, otherwise you will always be running to catch up.

The secret is all about presentation. You do not have to be a good technician to be a good businessman. You do need minimum standards, but you do not have to be brilliant. Of course, there are those that are brilliant and that is fine, but it is not prerequisite. In fact, technical expertise can actually hinder you, get in your way. So your background doesn't matter quite so much.

And what about your commitment? Can you add the magic needed to make a business really work under today's rules? It can be a very big world out there with everyone trying to be more successful than you. However, history is packed with people who have made a success of something. The rules for success are basically very simple – in fact the more you complicate them the harder business becomes.

All businesses go through four definite stages, and not to recognise that will cause strain, and can bring problems.

① During the first few years, no matter what success you have, money will always be tight and you will need to re-invest.

② Then your business, if it survives, will be ready to grow should you want it to. Again, money will be in short supply although you can have a few more luxuries.

③ It is in the third stage, when you have become established, that you can begin to enjoy the spoils of success.

④ Eventually, every business reaches the stage that, without some innovative thinking, it will fade and die. A serious danger for those new to business is to think that having got through the first phase you can take it easy. To do that only accelerates the onset of the final stage, and the third stage is missed totally.

The basic rules for success in business are:-

✓ *Stick to the knitting* – but first be sure you know the knitting pattern. Once you have got a good formula – stick to it. Develop a good business plan and use it. Do not try to change things just for the sake of it, although you must be aware that this needs balance. When things start to go wrong, find out fast and do something about it.

✓ *Ignore the idea of being best value at your peril* – to get and keep customers, they must see value in what you do or provide. Despite so many people talking about price as important (and yes, you must be reasonable), people buy on value.

✓ Be first, be right and *do things differently* from your competitors. If you do not stand out from the competition, then all you can do is compete on price – and that can only mean lower profits.

✓ *Competitive advantage* – develop it, exploit it and be sure to protect it. Be seen to be different from your competition in the way your customers want. Again, stand out from the crowd, do not be an also ran.

✓ *Never attack a brand leader head on* – build on your strengths and ride on the back of what the brand leader does. It stands to reason that leaders in a particular field get there because they are doing what people want. So let them advertise for you and pick up niche markets that are too small for the leader to be interested in. Or work with (or for) the brand leader direct.... Why not?

✓ *If you're not going to win, don't play.* Only winners will survive and prosper. If you are not going to win – there are no halfway stages. If you don't like the rules of the game don't play. But then, do not imagine that it all that bad – and there are people out there who can help if only you ask. Most people enjoy being their own boss and would have it no other way. Playing the game is fun.

✓ *How you get there is as important as arriving.* If you don't have staying power, forget it. Profits seldom come in the early years, and if you haven't set things up well, then, like a house of straw, it will soon come tumbling down.

✓ *Never start a price war unless you are sure you are going to win* – and price war winners are few (although there are many losers, which can be expensive and painful). The only real way to win via price is to invent a new way to do something so that the competition is at a real disadvantage. That comes through progress and by looking for new and better ways to cut costs.

✓ *Do not rob the business even if there is plenty of cash.* Build your brand name and share as the business grows, take the profit during mature and declining years – all businesses reach that stage. When a business is growing, you need the cash for growth and future prosperity in the majority of cases. One of the greatest limiting features is not having enough cash available when you need it – but there are routes around this if others can see you are not being greedy or stupid with money.

✓ The best time to stop competition is before it gets started – it's cheaper and easier. Play competition at your own game. Be better than they are. Know your strengths and play to them, and be sure not to open doors of opportunity for competitors by being ignorant or stupid – or playing straight to their strength.

Why do businesses 'fail'?

Many excuses – few reasons. When they do fail, most business people will want blame placed elsewhere. "It wasn't my fault." Yes, there may be things that haven't helped – there will be tough times economically, cheap foreign imports, lots of people cutting prices to try to stay in business (this is folly, as it seldom is a route to success).

You should be able to see tough times coming and act accordingly. Yes, occasionally things are beyond your control, but not that often. In the end it's all down to you. It is nobody else's business, nobody else's problem; it is down to you.

It reminds me of Lord Kitchener looking out of the famous World War I poster, pointing straight at the population and saying, "Your country needs ..."

Insolvency practitioners say the most common excuse is that the market has dried up. But why, when there are still many firms out there making money in the same market? Or it is claimed that it is lack of finance – well, that's a whole bag of worms, but if a company follows the basic rules, money is seldom a terminal problem, unless it's not realising you need it until it's too late.

From the outset, there are often fundamental flaws which are most often just down to getting the basics right. The cause of most business failures can be traced back to the boss. So here are two fundamental areas where you really ought to be looking for improvement in order to stay ahead of the game:-

1. **Know what it is you are going to do** – plan the future
2. **Stay in control** – know how well you are doing

Point the finger at yourself – that is the person who will stop your company going broke.

Value not cost

Compete on value. There is not much to be gained by setting out to undercut the rest on cost. Simply reducing price reduces profit, because your costs won't go down – indeed they may rise as you have to finance more sales. Everyone loses. Better to start with an idea, an approach or a service that will appeal to people, has value that is seen to be worth paying for. Think value, quality, and service ... not price. Competition on cost is folly for the smaller company – and for many larger ones as well.

Look at the consumer society in which we live. If price is so important, why do we still drive nice cars, wear fashion clothes, eat in smart restaurants, and want to buy quality brands? It is simple – what something costs is only really important when everything else is exactly equal, usually when you do not give any value to the package. It is my experience too. Once customers experience quality, be it service, taste, presentation or whatever, they come quickly to expect it. Who likes to think they can't afford, or don't deserve the best?

Marketing sounds really difficult, especially when you listen to marketing professionals. It is like nearly all specialist techniques – common sense with fancy words. Perhaps the easiest way to find out what people want is to ask them. Simple really, and asking brings with it the benefit that potential customers think that you are actually listening to what they want. The trouble with other people doing your marketing for you is that you lose that personal touch, and lose much of the benefit of the understanding that marketing brings.

Stay in control

You will never succeed unless you control expenses. My grandmother always used to say that if you look after the pennies, then the pounds would look after themselves. Never a truer word. When you start in business, you must remember that to survive will mean your controlling every cost. But on the other hand, you must not become an obsessive counter of beans, you must not let the control of expenses get in the way of building the business. Spend money wisely on those things you need, those things that matter.

Being in control of your business is a trick that is not as complex as it sounds. It does not require reams of paper nor endless computer printouts – quite the reverse. The human brain (unless yours is better than the average) can only take in and work with about eight or ten pieces of information at any one time. So do not flood yourself with facts. Make the figures really mean something. Too much information leads to inactivity – because of complacency or indecision.

'Turnover is vanity, profit is sanity', is a saying only too little understood by businesses. Success is often wrongly based on the size of turnover rather that the money that not only goes into the bank but stays there. To succeed in business is about a positive cash flow and profit. Better to be small and profitable than grow in size only to make less money.

Promises, orders, nice cars and fancy offices do make you feel good but count for nothing at the end of the day if you haven't got the cash to pay the bills, and many small businesses live virtually from hand to mouth. When creditors want paying, the trappings and promises mean nothing. Cash is king, and always will be. Very many new start-ups forget that not only will the business need funds, so will the person starting. The temptation is always to spend the money as it comes in rather than keep it under control.

I can remember that temptation myself – there were thousands of pounds in the bank, so why shouldn't I have a few luxuries when I worked so hard? It is not easy to say no, especially when your family sees the cash and you see them going without. It is sorely tempting to spend, but you must be cautious, at least when the business is young.

Self-management

There's only one of you, so value your worth and treat yourself well. If you don't, then no one else will.

Put a value on your time, and remember that it is important to keep quality time for yourself. Put a cash value on your time, which means that you can cost your contribution, and charge for it. Simply working long hours is not an answer. Doing extra work yourself is often a quick and simple route out of a current problem, but few times is it the right one. We still suffer the middle-class work ethic that says we must spend time at work, irrespective of what we do. Folly! As a result, a lot of businesses are held back because people like you spend all their time working *in* the business, no time working *on* their business, and leave little time for other things like family and friends.

Be careful to build enjoyment into what you do. If not, then the enthusiasm tends to wane. Find something you enjoy, even if there are aspects you dislike. Doing the bad bits is far easier if there are things you do like about what you do.

Your own personal management is very important. There is only a limited amount of time in the day, and when you start in business, you will find that there is never enough of it. To succeed will require that you spend time organising your day and week, so that the things that need to get done actually do get done. There is always something to fill your time. Many people find considerable difficulty in concentrating on what needs to get done. You will find that unless you get things done in an organised manner, you will be like a fireman – always going around putting out fires.

Profit is what is left over when you have paid yourself and covered your costs. Profit isn't what you live on. Pay yourself fairly, and then leave the profit alone. Only spend your profit very wisely.

When it all boils down to it, the reason we make the move to start a business is to make money. So, put simply, if you want to succeed in business, keep the turnover high, the bills small and make sure they don't exceed the income. If you don't spend more than you earn, you make a profit. If you spend more than comes in, then you make a loss. Simple, but very effective. So keep control of what you do.

There are few people who have the courage to make the effort – people like you – and these people deserve all the success and encouragement that they can get. So learn from this and from anything else that comes your way. Consider carefully what you want to do, with the clear intention of achieving it. The more you plan and think things through, the more you are in control of events and the greater your chances of making even an unusual business work.

Indeed, unusual ideas are often the best.

5

The Business Plan

One of the business fundamentals is knowing what you are going to do. It is your plan for the future. It is how your business is going to work! It's one thing to say, "I'm going to work for myself," quite another to do something.

Business Planning is about where you are and where you want to go. Planning gives you and others confidence and that confidence is based around the people that make things happen. So your business plan (or lack of it) speaks volumes about you and your chances of success.

The single most important thing in any business is the business plan. Most businesses say they have got one, although few actually do, and I see so many businesses that just drift along. When pressed, many business people say that their plan is in their heads, or that it was written for the bank to get an overdraft or a loan, or that it was written some years before, or even that it was started but never finished. Many, especially banks and accountants, see a business plan as just a cash flow with a few words. That is not a plan. We have the cart driving the horse here! The financial aspects of the plan are the result of planning. They are not the plan in itself.

I am often asked what are the pros and cons of business planning. Simple, with a good business plan, even an ordinary business can succeed, and without one, in time, all businesses will fail or, at best, go nowhere. It is a fairly simple philosophy, the pros are that the business will work, the cons are that it will fail. Simple really.

A business plan is simply a working action plan of what you are going to do, and how you are going to do it. The financial 'bits' of a plan are there simply to ensure that things are working out as you thought and are allowing you to stay in control. At the end of your planning, you should have not only a clear set of intentions, but also what specific actions are needed, by whom, by when.

So what about these financial bits that put everyone off the planning process? Well, they are no more than best estimates of what you think will happen if you achieve all you set out to do in your real business plan. You can start with an end in mind, but simply saying that you plan to sell £100,000 worth of goods does not give any thought to how you are going to do that.

I personally believe that many people are put off planning by the thought that you have to deal with complicated numbers, a myth perpetrated by accountants and big forms. It does not have to be complicated and you can put the numbers in whatever format suits you, as long as you understand what they mean. An example of perfectly adequate financial planning is given in Sharon's plan which comes in the next chapter.

How are you going to make those numbers happen?

Numbers do have a real advantage. If you can measure it you can manage it – if you can't, then you have no chance of achieving or improving. When you put numbers on paper, they take on significance and you believe in them. A business plan is a real document that must be picked up and reviewed as time goes on, so if things are going well, you can see why. But also, if things are not going as you planned, the earlier you know the better.

A major benefit of a business plan is simply the discipline of developing it, thinking things out. What should come out of a business plan is not some complicated document in its own right, but a catalogue of things you will do to make the future come true.

There are some people with an interest in your new business who ask for a business plan, indeed having a business plan is an essential part of their involvement. The most notorious are bank managers who seem to link business loans and overdrafts to business plans. "No business plan, no money". So plans often tend to be written with 'getting a loan' in mind. If you write the plan to bluff the bank manager, the only person you are bluffing is yourself. If the plan will not stand up without manipulation or an honest assessment, don't bother. You only fool yourself.

That calls into question most people's assumption of the bank manager as just being difficult and obstructive. Most of them want you to succeed, and a business plan is their only way of ensuring that you do. Equally, if they lend to you, and your business fails, then human instinct says that they do not want that failure on their record (without the proof that they have done all in their power to safeguard the bank's money).

? What obstacles do you see and how will you overcome them, by when?

? What will you do to market the business and sell your services or products?

? Yes, I understand that you have strengths, but every business also has weaknesses – just what are yours?

? And if you can see problems coming, just how are you going to overcome them? (This is not to put you off, it is more to make you realistic – and then do something positive about it.)

? And if things go well, where do the future opportunities lie, and just how will you realise them?

It does help to not let optimism overtake you. To keep a level head and to make a business go places, requires that you start thinking about the future as soon as you can. It is, of course, impossible to see into the future with any degree of certainty, but it is important to try.

Think the 'Big Picture'
A business plan tends to fall into very specific components, and often it helps to think first of the larger scheme of things. This is especially important early on when you need to think in the 'Big Picture', but is

difficult for many people who find detail comfortable, because that is what they are doing every day. Thinking in big pictures is disconcerting because it makes you question what it is you are doing and – heaven forbid – why you are doing it.

Do not be put off by what you think is impossible odds at this stage, simply think of what you want your world to look like, and what you want your business to be in say three, four or five years time. What sort of size, what sort of products, what kind of reputation, how many employees, what sort of premises, and so on.

Write things in personal terms (I am, we are) and write them so that you feel a part of them. If you do not believe in nor want this vision of the future, then what do you think will be the chances of your striving to achieve it?

Developing the details

The next things to develop are some reasonably broad views about how you will achieve this and by when. Just where does opportunity lie, and what can stop you getting there, and how you will go about achieving your aims. This 'Strategic Plan' is all about painting the main shapes, like plotting the route you will take on a major journey.

It is now that we can start to move into detail, and think about what we must do to achieve that grand plan. Be honest with what you think will be the outcomes of actions, and that if you think they will not do enough, then what more do you have to do. Only when you have exhausted your options should you consider looking again at your 'Big Picture' to see if perhaps it was a little too big.

Your dream is still a dream until you make it happen, and if no effort needs to be involved, then everyone would be doing it and it wouldn't be your dream! You have to keep the end in mind, all the time. A simple trick which I found works for me is to not merely to have a dream, but to imagine it is here and now, that I'm living it, that I can taste it and feel the excitement.

That brings two benefits, it makes me want to strive to achieve it and equally importantly it seems through some quirk of fate to bring its achievement closer to reality. Your dream must also have numbers so you can actually see your progress to achieving. An old phrase still holds true – if you can't measure it you can't manage it.

Never forget to reward your successes. When you achieve what you set out to do, then pat yourself on the back, even if it's only to recognise that you're part way there. Only too often people forget their successes, forget what they actually have achieved, so that their dreams never seem to be coming true. After a while, disillusionment sets in.

If you have employees, or are likely to have partners, get as many people's contribution to the plan-making as you can – this brings several major advantages. Everyone feels commitment even if his or her input has only been small. More heads see more issues, more options, other ways around problems, and take some of the stress and work from you. Many hands make light work. But most important, everyone knows what you are about – and why!

This is one of the reasons they say that the first plan should be not too ambitious – so that your first year of business gives you a success. Build the rewards into the plan. The financial aspects of a plan are simply a way of seeing if your business planning does what you want. If not, then I'm sorry, but it's back to the drawing board. A positive thought, however, is that, if you have to rethink your plans, then the financial bits will show you where more work is needed.

Perhaps the best known concern in business is money – usually never enough when you need it. But if you only focus on the money, then you become in effect merely a counter of beans. The money on its own *is* important, but I think it is something we put far too much emphasis on. It is people who matter most. Money is just a resource. If you've got the plan right, then the money should not be a problem as you should be able to access it or get people to support you. We will be talking about money in other sections of the book.

New businesses seem to get this bit about money all wrong. They always seem to need more money than they originally plan for. Certain factors seem to exaggerate this:

- sales are not as good as first thought
- sales are better than planned and they have to buy more raw materials – but will not get paid for four months instead of three

- they want a few extra bits of equipment, or since they first looked, prices have gone up, or technology has changed

- certain suppliers will not take credit – despite the new businesses' confidence – until they've proved themselves and have got a good track record, perhaps because they are having cash flow problems.

And so the list goes on – all signs of optimism that could have been foreseen.

So what can you do to keep cash flow positive?

There are only two real ways, (a) get the money flowing into the business, and (b) don't spend it quicker than it comes in. If a lot more goes out than comes in, you could have a problem. If it happens too much then you're in the mire. If you look around, then you will notice that successful businesses are careful about how they spend hard-earned profits. The signs are obvious when you look for them. Money is spent where it earns money.

Should you give credit?

In some industries you must offer credit, but build the price higher to allow for that. What you are effectively doing is lending your customers your money, and letting them build their business on your money. Mind you, if it's good for them, then provided you can get the credit, it's good for you too. The trouble is that by the time you've bought your stocks of materials, then made something, then been paid, and lived and eaten in the meantime, quite long times can pass between money flowing out and, it is hoped, more money flowing back in. There are two normal ways around this, arranging an overdraft from the bank and factoring (or invoice discounting). These are discussed later.

Overdrafts are never popular, surprisingly not even with the banks. The trouble is that they are built into the mythology of business life. However, they are becoming a thing of the past. Factoring is a good alternative and allows you to borrow the money against your debtors.

Pricing is always fun, and there is never a right answer – everyone has different ideas on how to charge. Built into your business plan should be a statement of what you will charge for your services and why. Most if not all people undervalue themselves, especially in the early years. You have to cover costs, pay all the wages – including your own – and still have enough to show a profit. Why should you charge less than others would?

Only you can determine the price you must charge, and certainly there are trends in the market that you must be aware of and might have to follow. If you start too low, the problems come when you have to raise prices later. Better to be able to reduce prices – it is always easier to think of excuses for that (and anyway people are usually forgiving when it's in their favour). Also you will find that people see a close link between price and quality even where that link does not really exist. So, if you decide to undercharge, be careful you are not seen as a poor quality supplier and manage therefore to 'shoot yourself in the foot'.

Pricing has a chapter all to itself later in this book – it is all about magic and mystique, and is basically a con. There are many who try to tell you of hard-won theories, but the best description I have heard of choosing a price is, "How long is a piece of string? Think of a number, adjust it, then that's your price." The magic of pricing is getting the price right, not just keeping price down. You are in business to make money. There are many pointers to the amount you should charge – do not be too greedy, but also do not be too cheap. Even the most scientific theories can backfire and how you determine price will in large part be determined by the business you are in. Just remember to charge for everything – every bit of the service you provide has a value and will cost you!

Writing the plan itself

What elements should your business plan cover? Even though the need for them is sometimes unclear before you start, looking back will show you why! They include:

- **History** – your background and why you have chosen to do what you intend. Why will you be successful? What marks you out as different from the crowd? What experience do you have? Why are you so confident of your success?

- **Your product or service** – what makes it special and unique? What is so special about what you do? Why should somebody, anybody, buy from you? What will you do to make the customer loyal to you? What makes you unique, stand out from your competitors?

- **Markets and sales** – how you are going to approach the market and how are you different from the competition? What are you going to do to communicate to the world at large to make them want what you have and, very important, what are you going to do to make them part with their cash? Include mention of advertising, PR, other promotional material, point of sale, backup, image, design – how do you plan to appeal and communicate to the market?

- **Operations and manufacturing** – how will you get product or provide the service – main points. How will you make things, how will you price things and why? This all boils down to how you are going to do what you do.

- **Management** – what management skills do you have or need, what are your beliefs, what do you bring, and how will you overcome any shortages?

- **Risks and rewards** – what are they and how will you both reduce risk and increase the rewards? Things will not be easy –they never are – and thought now can only make things easier later. Ask the 'What if?' question. Life has a habit of attacking you from behind, so if you've seen the problem coming and thought of what to do, then it won't happen. If it does, you know what to do.

- What are your **objectives and milestones** – what do you want from life and how will you go about getting it? What separates the achievers from the doers is that they recognise what they want. And remember, business life is not an end unto itself, it is only a route to allow you to do what you want.

- Analyse your **strengths and weaknesses** – this will indicate where future opportunities may lie as well as any threats. There are many things you are good at, as well as those areas where you are not so strong. Most people are negative and hence find themselves being reticent about their strengths.

- **Financial plans** – a planned income statement. What you think will be the income and expenses for the next two years if you do what you plan; cash flow to take into account any time delays in getting money in or paying money out; and any thoughts you may have on big capital expenditures. For this, the books and guides given out by the big high street banks are ideal, and if you have a computer, many now are putting the same service on disc to make it easy for you. There is a lot of free help with the financial aspects of business planning – there is no real excuse not to plan.

Beyond this, go to the banks, get their advice, see if anyone else can help (Enterprise Agencies, Business Links or Job clubs) and take your time in building up a good plan which honestly reflects what you believe could and should happen if you do as you say. I do see groups who think planning is a waste of time, but would you take two weeks off work without planning what you intend to do? Chances are not, even if you plan just to stay at home. Why should you approach the rest of your life with less effort?

Have your plan reviewed by an honest broker who isn't trying to sell you anything on the back of your work. There are plenty around who can help – even the local friendly bank manager – let them make comment. Be open. Go to someone who can question you, who will add value to your plan by asking you the kinds of questions you should be asking for yourself – just to see if you have thought of all the things you should. Speak to people who will help you see other, different aspects – but do not let them put you off, only let them help you to make your plans better, stronger, and more real.

Time spent now is time invested, time well spent, and not time wasted. If you have problems with planning, get help. If you hate finances, get help. Do not try to be clever and skip planning because you think yourself better or above it. There are a myriad books and several good computer packages available, and most colleges beyond further education run courses that include business planning. There is a stack of help. Use it!

6

A Real Start-up Business Plan

There is no set way to write a business plan and it important that the plan you make must be right for you. There are many different ways, and really it matters not a jot which way you choose. Every business studies course, every bank and most advisers have their preferred style. That can make it confusing, because everybody says theirs is the best way. Not true – yours is best if it really works for you.

To show it working in practice, I include a real example that goes all the way from how the idea started through to building some simple financial 'projections'. Nothing extravagant, this plan demonstrates how easy the business planning process really is when you're starting a new business. What I aim to do is take you through the thought processes behind the plans, show you that in reality, it's just common sense.

Everyone I have met hates the numbers associated with business planning. Very recently, I had a phone call asking, "Do you understand cash flows and profit and loss accounts?" I must admit my old headmaster and maths teacher had one very wise view. "Maths is there for a purpose, it is not there for it's own sake," he would repeat. I think it struck home because, from that time, maths lost its mystique. The numbers then became sort of logical. It's a bit like Margaret Thatcher and her analogy of household accounts – it is no more complex than that.

The person who wrote this plan, Sharon, was getting really fed up with working for someone else, even though she enjoyed the job. The boss, she felt, acted like an idiot. She could see the mistakes being made, where money was being lost needlessly. She felt it was time to do something for herself before the losses got so big she would be out of a job. Fairly 'arty', she is fascinated by colours and their use. She knew that if ever she were to start a business for herself, then she wanted to work in this field.

Sharon's first move was to get fully trained, completing the range of specialist skills she felt she would need to start. She was concerned, for her own peace of mind, that she could cope technically with a broader range of paint finishes. She took time out at work to practice and take advice, all the time knowing that one day she would be moving on, and one day soon. She felt that it was fair, and was later proved right, as the boss started to talk about cutting back on staff. He was losing money. Not a moment too soon, Sharon remembered the motto, 'Do It NOW!'

This longer-term view meant that Sharon could talk things over with her family and friends. Slowly her thoughts began to evolve, and what started out as an idea to specialise in complex paint finishes became a much more involved amalgam of selling services, advice, some limited range of specialist products, and acting as an agent for others in complimentary fields. But the idea itself was quite simple.

As the plan evolved, her thoughts become clearer, and Sharon took advice from her local Business Link. She also visited the bank and filled out their handwritten business-planning format as a guide. It forced her to structure her thoughts, that had so far been scattered and scribbled down on little bits and scraps of paper. Until that point, she could see too much opportunity and she had not picked on any one area and concentrated her attentions there – her business ideas had no form.

Step one was identifying clearly the nature of the business – just how would it specialise? In Sharon's own words, "Use a range of paint effects to enhance decoration and revitalise and/or sell furniture – at a profit. Will include sales of peripheral items and training courses. Makes and sell Rocking horses and kits." Sharon's exact words. Her vision was "To have happy and satisfied clients. Helping them with (my) skill with paint, and creative solutions for decoration and furniture." It is important to know that these are Sharon's words, in her writing, and she owns them … totally.

Rather than consider staff (something she didn't want, as she would rather work alone), Sharon went on to look at who would be important in her network for advice, for supply, as a source of work, and who would work for her as a sub-contractor – someone she could trust. She considered what she could do if she got particularly busy. Sharon is not silly, and realised that one of the keys to success is being able to get work. There was no point in just being a good with paint if she had nobody who wanted her to paint, so she saw a major part of her role as finding work and selling. This became an important aspect of her networking.

Next, she considered her 'Product or service and the market place'. In order of preference, Sharon listed all the areas she felt she could and would get work. Neatly, she had recognised that market forces would determine what she could charge, but had identified her niche as being not the top end of the market where she would need to have established a reputation, nor the bottom end where DIY reigned supreme. Sharon felt early that by addressing perhaps a lower level market than her ultimate ideal, she could get a good reputation quickly, and be busy in the meantime.

The business plan included the following phrase, based upon her direct experience gained working in a similar field. "Market size is unknown, but potential is very large." She went on to explore the geographical location, the earning capacity of likely purchasers and their preferences, and trends in the industry towards more personalised tastes. It all sounds complicated, but when you think about it, then it becomes common sense.

She had identified her client's needs as "Personal service, quality, service, flair and ideas, help, training and the ability to move with trends". We live in a fashion-conscious world. Sharon had identified that the market is shifting, with the cost of new replacement furniture being very high and the growing move to DIY solutions.

Sharon felt she would have no direct competition as she was operating in a niche market at the time, targeting mid-range clients. She identified all local competitors by name and their strengths and weaknesses – an essential first step in knowing how to deal with them. Oh, but business is fun.

Sharon had decided to use PR as the main source of publicity, and secured some help from her local Enterprise Agency. She arranged for two days training to show her how to develop articles the press would like and contacts into important media. She identified suppliers and the minimum range of materials she needed to stock, but picked suppliers that complimented her image. She developed her own packaging for some lines, and could charge premium rates just for this. (Having worked in the trade, she had seen some designers buy from her, repackage and more than quadruple the price to the end customer.)

In the matter of premises, Sharon was quite lucky. For her, premises were not a major issue; they were a place to advertise her skills, more real and effective than a box in a newspaper and less cost per week – even though she should sell from there. Sharon took part of a shop because the tenant couldn't use the whole space effectively. She received complimentary leads and the cost was very low, considering it included rates, electricity and services. This single cost made the idea of controlling expenses quite easy to understand.

Talking of expenses, Sharon was wise enough to realise that income in the first year was not likely to be excessive. She hoped she would be wrong, but was sensible to think that way. Because of this, she made one small mistake which could have been disastrous! How would she be paid? She would prefer to receive cheques or cash, but who carries chequebook or cash nowadays – it's all plastic. She felt at first that she could do without a land telephone line for credit card machines. Wrong in the longer term.

Other than this, things looked good. She would stick with the old car until she could afford the Jaguar. It was quite good enough, and low cost. Insurance she shopped around for. Her 'wages' or 'drawing' would be held at the same level as her current wages, £150 per week for part time work. Advertising (she would need some) would be one advertisement locally – £40 per week – and she would use an accountant to look after the books. Stationery and phone costs would be held down. Altogether Sharon felt she could hold expenses down to £365 per week.

In all this, Sharon felt she was lucky, and things just seemed to drop into place. In my mind, she made her own luck, and created conditions that let her proceed. Things do just seem to fall into place.

So what would Sharon sell? Obviously there could be no guarantee, but it was important to plan as best as she could.

1. Private commissions. Here Sharon felt that, to start, she could charge about £90 per day, and could get about 1 ½ day's work per week. £130 per week, say. Conservative, but safe. In the second and third quarter, this would rise to 2 days, say, £180 per week average, and this would rise to 3 days, say, £270 per week for the fourth quarter.

2. Furniture sales. Based at 50% gross profit, Sharon felt that she could act as an agent for some local pine furniture manufacturers, and would be able to make a commission. She selected her suppliers well, and picked lines that traditionally move quite well. Also she had interest to spend 'idle time' working to add value to either new or older pieces.

3. Rocking Horses. Sharon felt that in the three months running up to Xmas she would sell six horses, about doubling her investment to have them made (they are her own design and construction).

4. Courses. This would be an important generator of cash especially in tough times. Everybody wants to try the new, and especially in the specialist decorative field. Sharon felt that to allow £50 per week (as income after all costs of staffing and materials) would be fair. From her last employer, she felt she had taken many ideas allowing her to put on courses better than he had.

5. Sales of ancillaries, paints, brushes etc. At a 50% gross profit, Sharon felt that she could generate quite a nice regular income.

6. Fill-in work. Being sensible, and not wanting to lose contacts, Sharon decided to work in a friend's lighting shop one day per

week. If nothing else, the income from this would just about cover the cost of the shop – well, almost.

So, this brings us to her planned income. Sharon saw it as important to formulate a rough idea at least. Her estimates are shown here. Turnover (sales to you and me) is expressed as T/o, and gross profit as GP

	July, August, September		October, November, December.		January, February, March		April, May, June	
	T/O	GP	T/O	GP	T/O	GP	T/O	GP
Commissions	£130	£130	£180	£180	£180	£180	£270	£270
Furniture sales	£200	£100	£400	£200	£200	£100	£400	£200
Rocking horses (ave)			£400	£200				
Courses	£50	£50	£30	£30	£100	£100	£100	£100
Ancillaries	£40	£20	£60	£30	£80	£40	£80	£40
Fill-in work	£40	£40	£40	£40	£40	£40		
Totals	£460	£340	£710	£880	£800	460	£850	610

So, Sharon calculated that, as far as she could tell, in the first quarter she would make £340 gross profit a week, £680 a week in the second quarter, £460 a week in the third quarter and back to £610 a week gross profit in the last quarter. Easy really.

That's just on paper, but it was Sharon's best guess, and you've got to start somewhere. Yes, I know reality will never look just like that, but if you don't have a plan, then you're going nowhere. If you haven't thought about going somewhere, how will you know if you are going wrong? The numbers will just become a guide.

Cash flow would be easy, because Sharon would be dealing mainly with the public, and she would be paid as she either parts with goods or provides a service. It is a bit different dealing with industrial customers, and you need to be aware that the money you plan to earn may not come in for months.

Let's look at how this would span through the year. If I assume that Nostradamus was wrong, and the year has 52 weeks, then each quarter has 13 weeks. In practice Sharon will have time off for holidays and breaks, so let's say she will work 12 weeks a quarter, 48 weeks of the year.

1st Quarter	12 weeks	@ £460 per week	= £5,520 per quarter
2nd Quarter	12 weeks	@ £1,110 per week	= £12,320 per quarter
3rd Quarter	12 weeks	@ £600 per week	= £7,200 per quarter
4th Quarter	12 weeks	@ £850 per week	= £10,200 per quarter

Total income for the year = £36,240

1st Quarter	12 weeks	@ £340 per week	= £4,080 per quarter
2nd Quarter	12 weeks	@ £680 per week	= £8,160 per quarter
3rd Quarter	12 weeks	@ £460 per week	= £5,520 per quarter
4th Quarter	12 weeks	@ £610 per week	= £7,320 per quarter

Total gross profit for the year = £25,080

So now we can see what the business is going to earn. It will not make her into a millionairess yet, but it is at least a good start.

But what about expenses? We all know that even when you are not earning, you have to spend. So Sharon's outgoings, her expenses, will carry on for 52 weeks of the year. Let's assume that Sharon has got it right – her expenses will be about £365 per week. This is probably a bit high as already she knows that she has over-estimated for insurance and a few other items, but she has not allowed for a fixed telephone.

1st Quarter	13 weeks	@ £365 per week	= £4,745 per quarter
2nd Quarter	13 weeks	@ £365 per week	= £4,745 per quarter
3rd Quarter	13 weeks	@ £365 per week	= £4,745 per quarter
4th Quarter	13 weeks	@ £365 per week	= £4,745 per quarter
Total expenses for the year = £18.980			

Expenses will be level, but we can see that Sharon's expenses for the 1st quarter will be more than her income. So, she will either have to beat her expectation of sales, or she will have to get access to some money. If she is careful, when she starts, Sharon will have to understand that she needs £700 more money just to keep going. Given that Sharon estimated that she would need £3000 to start, she was able to go to the bank and start to negotiate a loan. The bank recognised the detail of her planning and felt confident to lend her the £3000, and suggested she should have the facility to have £2000 on overdraft, just to cover the shortfall planned and in case she needed a bit more. By doing it this way, Sharon did not over-borrow, important for a smaller concern.

That is really all there is to it – finances – really no more than that unless you need to make it more complicated. Sharon really did understand her plan, and how the numbers were brought about. Whether she does actually control her business is another matter altogether, because it is only too easy to get too involved with the work. Last time we spoke, Sharon was so busy in one area that cash flow should not be a problem.

The next section of the book deals with the important issue of how you make sure that your best intentions become reality. This is the stage Sharon is at at the time of writing. She has got going and is doing better than planned. The great temptation is to spend the extra money, but that is folly, because you need caution at this stage. Build up reserves so that when opportunity comes, you can grasp it. That enables your business to grow.

7

Get Control

Keeping your finger on the pulse of the business is what will make a major difference between success and failure. It will help you to:

☑ **maximise your profits**

☑ **control your cash**

☑ **allow you to grow the business more quickly and more safely.**

It is difficult to be successful but it is a lot easier when you know what is going on, when things happen and if they are as you want and expect. The pressure on you seems to lessen and you will seem to spend less time going around putting out fires. Equally, by dealing with a few important numbers, you will not have to spend time confronted by a mass of financial information. If, like me, you hate unnecessary numbers in lists (with money signs on them) and too much detail, when faced with a set of accounts you will not even see the problems – not without spending a great deal of time which could be better spent.

So, keep control of those few important numbers. Don't just leave them to the accountant or the bank manager – which is like putting your business in their hands. Not good. Without personal control, you lose that intimate understanding of how your business is doing, if it is profitable, if there are problems coming, if you have enough cash to pay wages or buy stock, or whether you can pay the bills at the end of the week. And if your business is doing well, and you are growing, surely you will need to know if you need extra money, and from where. Do not be too busy to know how well you are doing – that way you can become a busy fool.

There are several basic rules that must apply to controlling a business, which many people just seem to forget. These are:

● Never try to have too much information – 8 to 10 key numbers or bits of information are enough, provided you know what those numbers mean if needed (more on this later).

● Make sure, if things are not going well, you do not put off vital action.

● Review your information as often as needed, but certainly regularly and never less frequently than monthly (for important stuff – read weekly)

● Be sure the information you use is right – all else is madness.

Control must always be on key items, never on peripherals. It sounds simple, but knowing what is essential is often not that easy. Often, what you need to control gets confused. A good reminder goes back to the root of what business is all about ... profit. How often I have seen companies judge success against market share or turnover and make a loss, when reduced turnover (and the implications of size) would have brought them a profit.

It is impossible to create a generic list for all businesses, there are sure to be things to control for a builder (for example) that are different for the corner shop or a hairdresser. But even so, there are rules and ideas that must hold true for all businesses – and these are often the very things that are overlooked. These could include:

● break-even sales – just how much you must sell to cover all your costs
● major cost elements (for example wages and overtime)

- productivity – how efficient you are at using staff and your time
- gross margin – how much you make on each item
- cash – can you pay the bills
- debtors, and their age, and creditors as well – can you pay the bill
- stock (including work in progress) – have you got too much money tied up here, as stock is not always so good
- sales (goods out the door and hence money coming in – not orders), because money coming in pays the bills
- who in your business is doing what – action speaks louder than words.

Break-even Sales

This simply means the sales you need to cover your costs. Knowing this actually helps you to get the most from your business – or minimise your losses – by focusing action. Making a profit means that your sales are above break-even, making a loss means you must be below break-even, or just 'breaking even' means that your company is treading water.

A simple example may help. To understand this we need to know some simple self-explanatory terms.

1. *Sales* – the amount sold.

2. *Variable costs* – the costs that vary directly (well just about directly) with sales. Examples are cost of products you sell, transport costs, wages of people who work on the thing you sold (but not staff unless they are paid on commission). There are others but you get the idea.

3. *Fixed costs* – the costs that stay the same whether sales go up or down.

4. *Gross Margin* – the difference between the value of sales and how much those sales have cost you directly. This can be described in cash terms (£ or   if you are really trendy) (the Gross Margin) or as a percentage of sales (the Gross Margin Percentage).

Before you can work out your break-even, you need your gross margin. Sorry, but I'll use a few numbers here as an example to help explain what I mean. It is easier then, and explains itself.

Sales	£ 5000	
Variable Costs	£ 3000	
Gross Margin	£ 2000	(5000 – 3000)

The Gross Margin Percentage is $\dfrac{\text{Gross Margin}}{\text{Sales}} = \dfrac{2000}{5000}$

$$= 40\,\%$$

The Gross Margin Percentage is 40 %

Assuming your fixed costs are £1600 (leaving you a net profit of £400 i.e. £2000 – £1600), your break-even sales (the sales you need to break even) can be calculated by dividing your Fixed Costs by the Gross Margin Percentage.

In this example, with fixed costs of £1600 and a Gross Margin Percentage of 40%, the break-even point will be:

$$\frac{£1600}{40\%} = £4000$$

This means here you have to sell £4,000 of goods just to break even.

So how can you use this information? Well, to improve, of course. Obviously you can increase your sales, but as we know this does not necessarily mean more profit as you may increase costs correspondingly. But there are certainly routes to take.

● It is great to improve sales if your break-even sales point stays the same, but as you increase sales, your costs may well increase – more staff, more cars or vans, costs of borrowing go up, as may storage costs (at least costs may go up in the short term and leave you dangerously short of cash).

● You could reduce your variable costs by finding cheaper sources, or control costs better (try even not incurring some of these costs in the first place, like unnecessary visits), thus increasing Gross Margin.

- Fixed Costs could be reduced by cutting overheads – often not quite as easy as it sounds, as these are often the first to go in times of trouble.

When you know your business and your break-even sales, you are certainly in a much better position to make decisions.

In the example above, the position could be much improved by a small improvement – say, variable and fixed costs are reduced by 5 %. Variable costs are now reduced to £2850, and fixed costs to £1520. How will this impact your company?

Gross Margin becomes	£ 2150	(£5000 – £2850)
Gross Margin Percentage become	43 %	(£2150 / £5000)
Break-even point becomes	£ 3535	(£1520 / 43%)

A small improvement in cost mean you can get by with a major reduction in sales. If you keep your sales the same and reduce costs, just a small amount, profit rises significantly. It could mark the difference between success and failure! In this example it shows a small cost reduction will mean you start making profit much earlier.

Gross Margin

The aim is to get the best Gross Margin. It is, as you realise, the essential first step on the road to making a profit. It is the profit generated from trading which allows you to pay other fixed costs (rent, rates, salaries, telephone, cars, meals out) and, ultimately, your wages.

Your Gross Margin is therefore effectively the same as your Gross Profit, and is bound to be a key piece of information. With a low Gross Profit, making a Net Profit after expenses have been paid is difficult. With a good Gross Profit, you stand a chance. A good Gross Profit and a poor Net Profit (the bit that's left at the end of the day), can only mean your overheads are too high. Look at salaries of staff for the jobs they do, the costs of premises – do you live too grandly – or the costs of financing the business (including bank charges) which quite often are high if you started without enough capital. These can be killers!

Major cost items

There will be several major cost items that you have more control over than others, and these typically are around wages and numbers of staff. Every unnecessary expense has a disproportionate impact on the business, as we saw in the break-even point.

There will be major areas where small decisions, however unpopular with staff, will have major impact.

It is more important to control these than the costs where improvements are likely to have small effect. It all boils down to percentages and value for effort, but is not restricted to wages. Purchases can bring significant improvements too, often indirectly. Changing the way things are done may even remove costs from your accounts while there may be a small increase in the purchase price. It is up to you to explore, experiment and understand. A good example, fashionable since the early 90s is outsourcing, where you actually purchase elements of your service from specialists. The advantage is that it allows you more efficient use of the resources you use.

Productivity, a taboo word?

This I loosely translate as 'what you get for what you pay'. You want it to be fair, reasonable, improving, better. Staff traditionally have seen productivity improvements as trying to get more work done for the same pay – you being unfair by asking them to actually work for a living. But it also applies to your efforts, are you getting the right return for them.

This is unfair in the way it is phrased, and is designed to be so. It deliberately provokes emotion because in sharp black and white terms, the only way you will ever improve productivity is to look at it totally dispassionately. And that must be one of your aims as it directly impacts on costs (variable and overhead) and therefore profitability. It can mark the difference between success and failure. It is what determines the relative size of your wages bill, and how much you can get done in what time.

In fairness to the vast majority of people, most workers and staff like to give what they see as a fair day's work for a fair day's pay. What they see as fair may not be the same as you, and people perform best under a bit of pressure.

The subject of productivity is not just about slave-driving, nor is it about treating staff badly. It is the whole area of getting more out of every pound spent on wages, for every hour spent working. It is about working smarter, possibly outsourcing, using new methods and technologies, and doing things differently. By improving productivity it can give a major advantage against firms who resist change. It is also a major benefit of being small, where size matters in your favour!

Cash – it is king after all

Cash is the amount of money you have at any one time to pay your bills. It is not profit. It is the cash you can get your hands on at any one time without taking out new loans. That could include 'cash', overdrafts, loans not yet used and (if you use factoring or invoice discounting) your debtor book. Cash is really the only thing that we can use to pay our bills – the days of barter are no more in real terms. If you cannot pay your bills, your creditors (those people you owe money to) will not really care how profitable you are, they will want to be paid simply because their business depends upon your paying.

Debtors are the main flow of cash into the business, and creditors the main outflow. Any stock is dead money sitting there – so keep it to a minimum. There are other flows in and out, but debtors, creditors and stock are the traditional three main components of what is known as 'working capital'.

Your aim is to ensure that the right amount of cash is in the right place at the right time. Too much in any one place causes problems. Too many creditors may (and do) stop you buying, so you stop trading unless you can either pay them or find product elsewhere. Have too many debtors and you stand the risk of losing your money, or you have to pay interest on an overdraft to stand the debt. Too much stock is just money sitting there – and it could become obsolete (and therefore worthless) very quickly.

Debtors and Creditors, two key numbers

There are a number of ways you can improve your position. These are common sense.

- Take up credit references – not as difficult or costly as it sounds.
- Ensure customers know your terms and conditions.
- Do not forget to send invoices – ask to be paid – and get the details right.
- Be careful of key dates (like the last day of the month being a cut-off point).
- If you are promised a cheque, follow it up.
- Keep records of outstanding credit.
- Either charge persistent late payers or give early payment discounts.

Remember that these 'tricks' will also be used on you if you are a poor payer. The situation is more serious though where you are owed large amounts of money, especially by a few large accounts (80% of your debts will be with 20% of your accounts). You are in effect financing them to be in business, they are using your money as cash in their business.

Equally, long-term debts are much more likely to go bad. Poor payer are poor payers because they do not have cash to pay you (in the majority of cases). The longer you leave a debt, the greater the risk.

A trick used on a few councils and other large companies is to recognise that they pay on (say) the third invoice. Try sending an invoice every week rather than every month as they assume you will do. See if it works, it probably won't, but it just may!

Stock

You really do have to control this, it is absolutely crucial – especially in a world where the pace of change is growing. To make to stock is becoming dangerous in even traditional industries. Yes, build common components in advance, but as customisation and choice is becoming the norm, to return to the philosophy of Henry Ford (where you could have any colour as long as it was black) is madness. So know what your stock is, against specific orders if they are large enough, but at least keep a track of what money is lying around dormant.

Sales (and orders if there is a significant lag between them)

Ultimately, from break-even you must be keeping a weather eye on turnover. It does sound obvious, but it is so seldom done. Many companies ignore sales information – to their cost – and many just complain of 'a bad year'. If you know details of your sales, and armed with break-even figures, you can then cut your coat according to your cloth. You can start to control expenses. You can give priority. You can act.

Perhaps the first place to start is with targeting. Set targets for those people who have a responsibility for bringing in the business. You depend on it. If you do not give it high enough priority, then you cannot expect your staff to either.

There is a strange correlation between your keeping control of sales targets, and those targets being achieved. Even if you are the only person out there selling, this is what is planned, and this is what is happening. The result is either, "I'm on target," or "I'm below target, I'd better do something about this." Do not compromise with this area and do not accept just 'it feels good' control – ask for absolute numbers. Good prospects are not sufficient, what you need is confirmation of actual sales or orders or money in the bank.

Keeping control – the numbers game.

Obviously, when running a business there are some numbers you must know. A combination from the list above will comprise numbers from the accounts (all computer accounts packages can get a variety of these) and operational information. Look at these numbers, use them as you feel best to get the most value from them, but use the numbers. If you use numbers then you can compare like with like, see trends, see improvement or problems coming.

If you have no numbers, you quickly get into a woolly environment where staying in control is like trying to run in wellington boots –

difficult and not very successful. Numbers say it all. But which numbers?

The start of it all goes back to the business plan – what you felt you would do and the financial statistics that would result. So your business plan must include the numbers you will be controlling against. What did you plan your break-even sales to be? What of Margin? What stock? Obviously you will have built several figures into your cash-flows, items such as major costs, cash, debtors and creditors and sales.

So the starting place for control is your business plan and the numbers you believed would happen. The numbers you control then must reflect this. The business plan gives you the target, the plan, and you should control the actual results achieved, the things measured.

All the banks produce documents and systems to help you get control of your business, even though bankers are not businessmen. These ideas will help – for many small businesses, they will be more than adequate. Most crucial to control is cash-flow and banks produce a simple set of charts to help give you a useful comparison of expectations against what actually happened. There is no point making it too complex. It is far better to keep the system simple and use it than complex and not.

If things are going well, how can we improve upon them (because in business as in life, we should always endeavour to improve). If things are not so good, then what must we do to get back on track. Where did we go wrong, and is there anything we can learn?

There is no point being in control unless you generate and focus action, do something to enhance or improve your position. In small businesses, that will often mean that it is down to you to change the way you do things. In bigger, better-established businesses, this often means getting others to do things differently. In both cases you need action and that means an action plan – who is going to do what, why and by when. Keep it short, sharp and to the point.

Maintaining control brings focus on Kipling's 'honest serving men' again ...

<u>What</u> you need to do,

<u>How</u> you need to do it,

<u>Where</u> you need to get it done,

<u>When</u> it needs to be done,

<u>Why</u> you need to do it or do anything at all,

and

<u>Why</u> you need to do it in the first place!

8

Sources of finance

Money is the oil to make the gears and machinery of business work. Not enough, and the whole thing makes grating noises, and sometimes business just grinds to an abrupt and untimely halt. Too much is seldom a problem, but like oil in a machine, too much money seems just to splash around and stick to things where it isn't needed and has no real effect. Too much money gets wasted, and can make your business sluggish.

Money is also a subject that everybody fights shy of, and that is a shame. You do not need to be a whiz-kid, but in business you do need a basic understanding. It increases your options. Many people starting out see money (or lack of it) as the reason not to do anything.

This chapter will outline the main sources of outside finance, and some of the pros and cons of each option. Equally, if you decide to go down any of these routes, there are pointers as to how best to approach any lender, the most common being the bank. The financial world is one where, if you are not expert, you should take advice. It is worth it in the long term.

Do not think that it is hard to get hold of money if you are looking to start a business. There is a lot of money sloshing about, and stacks of people just dying to lend money to deserving causes, of which you are one. It is a crazy world, but the way the financial world works is that the more money a bank lends, the more money it is able to lend. They want to lend to you, as long as that debt is reasonably secure.

Obviously the cheapest and most cost effective source of money is that which you put in yourself, or that which the business generates itself. This seldom has obvious costs, and consequently allows you to undertake things that other people would not support. There is a big question here as to whether you should apply similar disciplines as you would for external finance. If I had done so, then one of my past ventures would have been left well alone. Some lessons do not come cheap! Even if you have bags of money, this would be a good chapter to read. Odd, but when people have ready cash, they do not seem to be so careful how they spend it.

Before we look at the various source of finance, let's take a quick look at what you need money for, whether you need finance, and if so, what sort of money it would be reasonable to expect to borrow.

Why will you need money?

Silly thing to ask really, but do you really understand why you may need money, and how much you will need? There are start-up costs and no business is really successful straight away. Some businesses generate income from day one, and sometimes you either buy an existing business or are almost handed a business on a plate. These examples are few and far between, and even they can run into problems with money.

Your business really determines how you operate, and the amount of cash you need.

- You may need *facilities, a shop or premises.* Most of these suppliers or services will require an up-front commitment, a deposit. You may need a painted sign, perhaps decoration, and certainly you will require cash for these.

- *Printing* is another hidden cost, for cards, brochures and perhaps a letterhead. Again this will need to be paid, and you will need cash here, as few people will give credit at this stage.

- There will be *organisational costs* too at starting up – the cost of setting up a limited company (not for everyone), buying packages for accounting, and perhaps getting access to advice.

- One of the major outgoings is for *equipment*, and you alone know what you may need. Industrial quality equipment is not cheap – it is significantly more expensive than domestic quality – and you must know what you want and how much it will cost. It can come as a nasty shock. It may be possible to lease, locking you into paying the costs through the time you use the equipment. These options are described later. There are cheaper options, and paying cash is always the cheapest way. Second hand or bankrupt stock is a great way. Equally I would advise caution, as many people rush in and buy things they will seldom use – things which may be more cost effective to hire. Do you need the equipment more than you need the money?

- *Cars, vans and trucks* can also become an expensive commodity. Explore leasing, HP, and even buying second-hand. The implications are that differing routes require different kinds of money and can significantly alter the cash you need. The same applies to much of a company's equipment – there are finance options that you should explore. It transfers the need for money from payment up front (cash, where are you going to get it?) to payment out of normal cash flow.

- *Operational finances* also will vary with need, and will depend upon what you are doing. Here need for money up front will change and there is usually considerable latitude in how you finance. Many suppliers are only too happy to help and will give you some credit. In some industries, there is little chance – for example catering, where you will have to find the money for all of your stock at the time.

Certain costs need to be carefully considered. These include:

- *Staffing* – If you employ staff, they will need to be paid weekly or monthly and that money will have to be 'in the bank', otherwise your workforce and company will just seem to melt away. Staffing is always a very big cost, and is always more than you estimate!

- *Her Majesty's Government* – Its various forms or agencies (Inland Revenue, VAT, and Contributions Agency) are all in the background. These are never the best people to cross, so if you need to set aside money for these, do so. Do not get caught in the trap of hoping to find the money elsewhere later. Some do, but the penalties for late payment can be draconian.

- *Local Government* – Things like business rates and various permissions or licences (it seems like you need permission to breathe sometimes) all need to be considered in cash requirements.

- *You* – Life is not really that romantic, and you will need some money for yourself. No good starving! Yes, you can live on credit cards, but these must be paid back sometime, and the mortgage or rent must come close to the top. Not considering your own needs is silly. If you run out of money to pay personal bills, then it can create havoc for the business.

  The problem is County Court Judgements (CCJs) and the legacy they leave. If you have CCJs against you, getting money now or in the future becomes more difficult, no matter how small the sum the CCJ was awarded for.

Obviously, the sooner you can get to a positive cash flow generated by sales, with your customers actually paying, the better. Lack of cash is sometimes a benefit, as it motivates you to get out and sell. Too little though, and you spend your life and your attention juggling money.

Be creative in what you see as your money needs, and if you juggle the way you get the things you need through leasing, finance and debt (as well as money you bring in), then so much the better.

The trouble is that, when you start out, you will probably not have the experience to understand all the options available. These are important, and their use will have serious impact on whether you do actually need someone else to put 'a hands in their pocket' to support you. The more common options include:

- Get better terms off creditors.

- Pay your bills later, often an opportunity but never pushed too far because it's seldom explored. It is a cheap option, but like anyone else, your suppliers are keen to get hold of their income as soon as possible. With a new account, they are often loath to be too generous with terms.

- Credit cards – virtually everybody understands the availability of credit via cards, but if you only need a small amount of cash for a short time, this is often an easier and cheaper option than a loan. Most new businesses have a separate bank account and getting a business credit card with access of between £500 and £1000 should not be too much of a problem.

- Lease and hire purchase – these are for the big bits of kit.

Let's face it though, when you start out, the chances are that you will want some money from somewhere. There is money to help business, and the financiers are looking to help. The problems of a good business getting support are never insurmountable. Financiers know whether they will support a plan before it gets to the amount of money you need, and if it's going to be 'no', then they know before they get to the financing.

Should you be looking to borrow, and how much?

Your own personal circumstances determine whether you need to borrow, but certainly you will have to put some of your own money in, under the majority of circumstances. As a guide, anyone putting money into your business will be looking for you to show that you are committed to the business, and that if the business goes 'belly up', then you also stand to lose. That way you are less likely to let things go wrong. Without that finance, people become cautious. Very Cautious.

The starting point for the bank manager (the most common sort of person to help) is to look at a one to one ratio of money you put in to that which you borrow. He'll match what you can put in. But that's only the starting point, not a hard and fast rule, and always he is willing to go much further than that, provided that he doesn't think you'll be trying to make a fool of him.

It all depends upon the nature of the business, the amount cash you will need, and the reason you want to borrow it. If, perhaps, you are looking to borrow all money to start, he may look at security. When one of my favourite managers saw this, he remarked that no bank acts as a pawnbroker. But security does demonstrate your commitment – that is perhaps why banks don't like the government backed schemes (more of this later), as they take away the personal commitment to avoid losses.

A cautionary note. Money is only a relative measure – the more you borrow, the more you have to repay, and the bigger the ongoing costs later. It's never a problem at first, but it does become onerous as time passes and you have other uses for the money. It is for this reason that the banks and financiers prefer there not to be too much dependence on borrowed money when you start.

When you've been in business a while, there is more reliance on borrowed money, and cash flow becomes almost the most important thing to worry about.

Fewer and fewer businesses ask for help at start-up. Many new businesses find enough money themselves, either from their own resources or from other options like leasing and credit, but not all do. Almost three-quarter now use all (or very nearly all) their own money, whereas 10 years ago most people went to the banks for help. Do not let this statistic stand in your way, as everyone's circumstances and needs vary. It makes the banks that bit keener to lend.

If you've got a bright idea but no funds, do not expect an easy ride. Investors are often difficult people to part from their money if you have absolutely none. They like to see a good track record and some kind of confidence that the business will work. Market research, potential clients and the reaction of alternative lenders will help. The more of your own money you can commit, the more confidence you will inspire.

Assuming you still feel you need access to money, where can you get it, what are the sources?

Let's look at them.

£   *The Bank* – Probably the best known establishment on the high street and the people we all seem to be working for. Not as unfriendly as you may think, provided you play the game their way! They have two real forms of money, longer-term debt such as a loan, or short-term debt ... the overdraft

£   *A friend or acquaintance* – Often called a business partner, whether in the true sense of the word or not, this can be a friend, business colleague, parent or other family member. This is most often invested in the form of equity, where you are giving away some of the ownership – you are selling a stake in the business in return for the money they put in to help get you started.

£   *Grants* – We have all heard of them, and many people tell tales of buckets of money being splashed around. How can we find these buckets?

£   *Leasing and Hire Purchase* – The dreaded HP is more common than you would think and comes at you under various guises. It has got to be considered when buying big items.

£   *Factoring and invoice discounting* – This is sales ledger financing, effectively borrowing again your sales ledger, often a taboo concept but with much to offer. It can be a great source of money if you are growing the business quickly, selling loads of stuff but are having problems getting hold of the working capital to pay the bills.

£   *Venture capitalists* – These are people with money to spend who are looking for a high return for their investment, are willing to take risks and are looking for a short-term ownership stake. Because of this, they are very picky about the businesses they invest in – it is not for those businesses that do not plan to grow very quickly, but you can make a lot of money by this route!

£   *Business Angels* – These folk are much the same as venture capitalists but offer smaller amounts of money and interest in the business itself. They also add advice.

73

Banks – the final frontier!

Banks are a business, and their business aims to make profits out of helping you meet your aspirations – and your need for money. They want to do two things, lend you money and sell you financial services linked to that. If you follow a fairly basic set of principles, almost anyone with a reasonably clean sheet should be able to access funds through a bank.

Banks are into 'relationship banking'. This is a jargon term put about by bankers, rather than say they are now more keen to understand you as a person – well as far as is possible, as far as is needed. Some managers are very good, many are less so. They have never experienced the world of the entrepreneur first hand.

To make life easy, there are some basics that need to be followed.

Approaching the bank

The following is a guide – not all banks want the same (they say), and no two managers are alike. The information a bank wants serves two purposes, to give comfort that you have thought things through and are in control of any risk, and to cover their backs if things go wrong. Bank managers are people after all.

Despite rumours to the contrary, most bank managers do live in the real world. Problems are most likely to arise with young, inexperienced bankers, who appear not to be able to see beyond the book of rules. Many exasperated businessmen unable to get what they want easily, and faced with a 'sprog' banker, throw up their arms in dismay. My advice is to see it from another's eyes, pander to them and win them over for the long term. Treat them well now, and you have a friend for life.

What is the bank looking for?

There are a number of things the bank is looking for:

- Personal integrity and suitability – your background, experience and resources. No point trying to convince them you're something you are not. A bank manager is more concerned with the person than the proposal.

- Justification for any loan – how much is needed and why, how this was calculated, the purpose of any money, the proprietor's contribution and the type of finance sought – loan or overdraft?

- How able are you to repay? This will be around cash flow, profits and the bank manager's view as to how realistic your plan is. What assumptions have you built into your figures? Try to be conservative as to what you believe will happen – bank managers are.

In all, if you do a good business plan, and bear in mind the advice in that chapter, you should have no real problems, although there can never be a guarantee.

Long or short term debt (loan or an overdraft)?
Banks at this level have two types of finance, although each have links which deal with the more specialist forms of finance discussed later. These are the overdraft or the 'term loan'; the latter so called because it is for a fixed term.

£ *Overdrafts* are the most flexible, the simplest but the most expensive. Interest rates are high, and many of your costs are hidden. They are also not really liked by banks because firms come to rely upon them. Overdrafts are being phased out (or so it seems). They are designed to cover changes in day-to-day costs, seasonality, for those who have delays getting money in, and for sudden, unexpected expenses. Banks like to see the overdraft come into credit as planned, and not used as long-term borrowing. It is not really an appropriate way for capital expenditure – buying big bits of kit you otherwise couldn't afford.

£ *Term loans* come under a multitude of guises, and each bank parcels them differently (although they are all basically the same). There is the traditional term loan, which has been the bedrock of bank lending for many years, the flexible business loan and a commercial mortgage. Term loans can be good for buying expensive equipment, business projects, vehicles etc., although a better form of finance may be HP or leasing (discussed later).

£ *Flexible business loans* differ in that they allow for capital repayment 'holidays' and the ability to defer repayments. Designed to reflect the slow start up of sales, most of the business start-up packages on offer from the bank allow for capital repayment holidays in one way or another. Banks are quite competitive, so go for all you can get!

£ *Commercial mortgages* (up to a maximum funding of 75% with some banks, but normally much less) have lower interest rates and are limited to purchase of property (but can be used to access cash through re-finance). There is a belief that the limit is 40% of capital outlay, which is rubbish. More expensive than domestic mortgages (but similar in main aspects), these are a cheap form of finance, so if you have money locked up in premises, it may be a way to release some.

Interest Rates
There are no set interest rates, but the guide is that they are between 2% and 6% over the base rates prevalent at the time. Unsecured rates are normally higher, 6% above base, secured closer to 3%. In financial terms, these are low interest rates, because the banks are not lenders against risky projects, even though we see these rates as extortionate.

Just what rate you finally pay is a subject of negotiation. If the bank wants your business, they will bring the rates down.

Bank managers have targets too, and you might be their target – do not forget that you have power. Below, say, 2½% is not possible for most managers to negotiate – that becomes a head office decision. You are normally doing well to get down to 3% above base.

There are fixed interest rates available over longer periods, but there are often penalties to come out, and I often question whether you gain significantly for all the extra agro! Perhaps with your home, yes – but your business?

Circumstances will change very quickly in business, and I don't see the point in tying yourself up just to save a few pounds.

Security

The needs for security differ whether yours is a limited company or whether you operate as a sole trader.

For a limited company, the bank will be much more comfortable lending if there are property deeds, insurance policies or stocks which have value. They may seek guarantees from you, or to take a debenture on the company. None of these is as onerous as it sounds, but, as in all things financial, take advice before signing.

For sole traders and partnerships, unlike companies, banks cannot take a formal charge over debts, and so may be keener to look for security – although it is not essential. At the end of the day, the bank is more concerned with the personal integrity of the person than the issue of security. You are important.

A final warning – all costs of the bank taking security are payable by the customer. This normally works out between ¾% and 1¼% of the total amount. So it need not be a cheap option.

Small Firms Loan Guarantee Scheme

A little gem, not pushed by most banks for reasons mentioned, is the DTI backed Small Firms Loan Guarantee Scheme (SFLGS for short). It is aimed at certain sectors, where there is a shortfall of available security, or no security at all. Suddenly an official loophole appears in the bank's insistence on security. But banks are not too keen, so it seems.

There are fine distinctions qualifying eligibility. As banks make decisions, and the system seems to be administered by banks, there is little consistency either between banks or between branches of the same bank. For established businesses, the limit is £250,000; for new businesses, it is limited to £100,000. Terms are for 2 to 10 years. Homes are not always counted as security – it depends upon your bank, and your particular manager. Get to know a friendly manager.

How good is your relationship with your banker? Should you start work on it? To enhance your eligibility, and because in business you need a friendly banker (because it is never black or white), go chat to a few banks. Your local Business Link or Enterprise Agency can help. Shop around. In my experience, bank managers are like anyone else, quite nice really, and it pays dividends to get on well with them. Be a friend when you don't need them, and they'll be good to you when you do!

Friends and Acquaintances

This is an area always fraught with problems. Where it comes to money, when things are going well, then the sun really shines. The trouble starts when things stop going well and problems arise, as they inevitably will. Money soon becomes a real test of friendship, and given the way many 'friends' react, bankers can appear quite friendly folk, despite their reputation.

Obviously the way to approach borrowing from family or friends, for your own piece of mind and future security, is to do it very professionally. Have some kind of an agreement signed by both parties, whether drawn up by a solicitor or not, which clearly lays out what each side will provide and each side will do. Do not let things be ambiguous. If there are any areas not sorted out they will come up and 'bite you in the bum' at some stage!

I have heard some dreadful tales. Stories of money promised then not delivered, money put into the business then demanded back only weeks later at no notice. Friendships, families and marriages breaking up over what in hindsight seem minor problems. Dreadful interest rates superimposed on the business after an amount has been agreed. Ownership passing from you, despite all your hard work in setting the business up! It can be a minefield and you are better taking advice before you leap in. Do not think yourself too clever, nor any friendship too strong – it may save the friendship at the end of the day to keep everything at a businesslike level.

I have also heard tales of successful businesses where acquaintances have invested money for a share of the business and left them to get on with it. The only cost has been to give away a part of the benefits (which in its own way caused minor resentment within the management). If you do things properly, it can work well for everyone.

Grants

Everyone thinks that there is someone out there with pots of money just for you to go and spend. In days past, that may have been the case and, if you watch the news, then it seems that if you are 'Johnny Foreigner', the government is only to happy to hand over large amounts of taxpayers' money.

Before we go much further, it is important to begin to understand what can be classed as a grant. No two grants are the same, and the many various sources of money have different systems for administration and delivery, which may or may not apply in all areas and across time. The major systems are:

- *Straightforward grants for business* – These are dollops of cash put into the pot when you can prove that a certain amount of work (for which the grant was awarded) has been done. These are mostly provided on a match-funded basis – i.e. you pay 50%, and the grant pays 50%. It can be 70/30, 80/20 or even 90/10.

- *Low interest loans* provided by certain groups in certain areas. An example was the then British Coal, who gave loans at a nominal interest rate in areas where pits had closed, far better than the banks, but which had to be repaid.

- *Help in kind, or the provision of expertise.* This is where agencies like the Enterprise Agency, paid for from the public sector, actually help you at little or no cost. Nothing is for free, it's just that you don't pay the bill, the exchequer does.

- *Grants to achieve specific political aims and initiatives.* Such may include European integration, green issues, social priorities in deprived areas, research into specific initiatives. You can benefit here more often by quoting for work funded by grants.

Grant aid depends to large part where you are situated. Contact someone like your local Business Link. They will have up to date information – the situation is very changeable. Business Links are often the only access to the most flexible forms of help.

Criteria for eligibility for grants can be a nightmare to follow, and will depend upon the specific grant itself. A few things can be taken as read. Application for grants is actually very time consuming, and you can spend a great amount of time in applying with no guarantee of success. Once you have been in business for a while, most people do qualify for assistance to help you grow the business by getting you specific expertise in areas where you need it.

There are a number of different types of grant. These include:

- **UK Government, and European money.** There are some pots of money to help specific areas. Qualification is always a problem, as is where to go for specific information. Business Link is a good first contact.

- **Single Company and Collaborative grants.** These are aimed at increasing integration and building upon common knowledge across Europe. These are often pan-European, and require several groups from differing parts of Europe to get together.

- **Local Authority grants.** These are not common unless you are in an assisted area. A good side effect is that local authorities are good at accessing money from other areas and this could provide local opportunity for work and business, even outside assisted areas. Go to them with ideas if you have any.

- **Business Links.** The grant help here is normally supportive, aimed at education and training or the provision of specialist advice and support. Often the aid these bodies give is in reducing the cost of business advice and training to make it affordable to those that most need it.

- **Export.** Always near and dear to our island is export help, and help to visit and research export markets. There are a number of schemes available, and this can include translation or help towards costs of researching export markets. Touch base with your local Chamber of Commerce or Business Link.

- **Start-up and business development.** There is no general financial support at the present, but there is help form a variety of sources to help companies. Various awards from certain bodies, such as the SMART awards or help from the Prince's Trust are always around, but finding current information can be difficult.

A note of caution! Beware of the taxman looking for people who have received gifts from afar! All grants are subject to tax I am informed by the Inland Revenue. Not all are taxed, but be careful how you do or do not tell the taxman.

There are many private agencies that go round touting for custom, which, for a fee, will guarantee to find you at least one grant. Beware. Often these charge up to £500, when you could go to your local Business Link and get the same service free of charge.

Leasing and Hire Purchase

This area is very confused, and the terms used don't really help. The brand names of various products are seemingly designed to confuse people, the best example being 'lease purchase' which is in reality a glorified form of hire purchase. For simplicity, and to avoid the pitfall of industry techno-babble, I will limit myself to describing the main options.

● Hire Purchase, or HP as it is better known, rose to prominence some time ago and, in doing so, because of the many abuses, got itself a bad name. Times have changed. HP is like a term loan with security taken on the thing you are buying. Very useful when starting up.

   There are several major advantages with this over leasing. With the final payment, you actually own the asset – it's yours. Consequently you can have any VAT and tax allowances, interest can be offset in expenses and you get to decide what to do with the asset. You also have to maintain it!

● Leases, on the other hand, have one fundamental difference. The asset is owned by the finance company, and the title NEVER passes to you. The Inland Revenue, who would see you as trying to fiddle your tax, forbids it. Shucks. The cost of using the item is therefore an expense, but you are never buying. This can make it a bit cheaper, but never much.

There are two categories of lease – finance leases and operating leases. These differ in one major way only. With the finance lease, you have the benefits and risks of ownership – if it breaks you repair it – whereas with an operating lease, you just seem to be renting the equipment over a fixed period of time. Operating leases (often called contract hire) are often used for vehicles.

Factoring and invoice discounting

This form of finance is best for established industries where there is a recognised delay in being paid, and for those companies who need access to these funds to be able to re-invest and grow. Unfortunately, during past times, borrowing against your sales ledger was used by many to buy time before closure, and now has a bad name as a result. It is not aimed to help failing businesses, but during times past was used to shore up failing companies.

If your bank manager advises speaking to a factoring company, and all banks have good links to one each, then take that advice and speak to them. Effectively, what you are doing is borrowing money against cash that will come in from goods that you have already sold and invoiced. With factoring, the finance houses chase the money. With invoice discounting, it is down to you, and you just get access to the cash. There is a stigma, but it is going.

When we come down to it, sales ledger financing (in its various forms) is nothing more than an overdraft, but using your debtor book as security. It is not cheaper than an overdraft, quite the reverse, but it does take away some of the work and gives you flexible access to your money. It is an alternative, albeit a very specialised form of finance.

But what happens if your customer doesn't pay? Well, it's your loss unless you pay a premium that in effect is insurance. Your business at the end of the day is your risk. Nobody wants to take that risk away from you. The greater the risks, the more you pay. The more you can do to lower risk, then, as logic would have it, the less you can expect to pay.

So, the good points. This form of finance does allow you to get on with business while those more able can chase your money. You can get the money quickly, up to 80% of invoice value within 24 hours of a sale, and if you are growing strongly the problem of overtrading is greatly reduced (running out of money because you are too busy so you cannot pay your suppliers or wages bill). When it all boils down to it, you get paid.

But there are two basic costs. There always are costs, and this is not cheap.

- There is the cost to you in interest on the money you draw down (you need not have it all) and this could be as little as 2 to 3% above base – the chances are it won't be.

- Then there is the service charge as they call it, which varies enormously – the price you pay for their administration.

There are no fixed charges, and like all commercial companies, if they want your business, they will bring charges down.

Remember that some of their charges save you work that you can devote to building the business. If you are interested in learning more about a complex area that can help, call your local bank manager, Enterprise Agency or Business Link.

Venture Capital

Venture capital is money committed to your business, enjoying equity participation, sharing the risks but enjoying the benefits. It is large amounts of money, probably starting at around £250,000, looking for a home where it can earn lots more.

But it is expensive, and the investor will be looking for about a 30% return on their investment for the risk they are taking. "What? 30 percent! That's extortion!" you say, to which they answer that it's the going rate, that nobody else would lend it cheaper, and it let you get your idea off the ground. It's better to have 70% of a lot of money, than 100% of not very much. They have a point!

It is not enough to go to your local friendly bank manager. He will not be able to think in numbers big enough. Speak to his boss or, better still, access some specialist advice from someone like Business Link as a starter. The way you start to go about accessing this sort of money is very different from the bank and they look for different things.

So what do venture capitalists look for?

To start, a good idea. Venture capitalists are looking for strategies for growth, and they need to see how you are going to control the business. Equally important is for them to see early on how they are going to get out – what is their exit strategy. They may think you marvellous, but they will not want to be with you for more than about three years – five at a stretch.

Theirs is a very little-known world. They are all nice people – except when it conflicts with being good business people. Get advice, and there are many places to go. Enterprise Agencies are normally out of their depth here. Do not let the distant image of high finance put you off, it is a world inhabited by real people. They just talk in big numbers.

Business Angels

Business Angels do not float about on clouds and have big white wings. They do not dispense fairy dust, nor are they necessarily nice. They do fill an important stage in the world of business finance. They are sometimes known as 'private investors' which is exactly what they are. Their name derives from 'Broadway Angels,' who financed major shows on Broadway.

All business angels are successful business people in their own right. Recent government tax changes have made it advantageous for them to re-invest in another business, and these kind folk are therefore looking to invest quite large dollops of money in high-risk businesses. But they do want rewards.

What do they want out of it? Like venture capitalists, they seek a high return in increased value of their investment tax free, and also the feeling that they have done some good.

For you, a side benefit of business angels is that they also bring networks of contacts and considerable skill (often in areas where they made their first nest egg). Often they will put in a certain amount of time to add real support. This can be a major benefit. A business angel's help is of enormous value, and they want to see you succeed because, if you do, then they do.

How much a business angel might want to invest depends upon how much money you want. It can be anything from £10,000 upwards. In reality, if you want smaller amounts than, say, £25,000, then your bank manager can get his mind and body around such numbers, so this is a bit too small. The majorities of investments are between £50,000 and, say, £200,000.

It is most important to remember is that these people, like venture capitalists, are not looking for interest, they are looking for capital growth. They will work with you for the long hauls – well, longish hauls. They will also not back off when the going gets tough.

£££££££££££££££££££££££

With this quick look at some of the sources of finances, I hope that you will at now feel more confident to ask questions of those who are there to give you help. And these are many. People who have dealings with business, from accountants to advisers, officials to those whose role it is to deal with money, are all there to help you explore the financial maze – should you want to.

These people are like you and me, but they have done one thing that is absolutely vital. They have ceased to see a lack of money as a reason not to do something; they have seen money as a resource to help them get where they want to be. Whether from the bank or the city, people are there to help you. If you want to do it on your own, then that is your choice. There are alternatives that you would do well to explore. I hope that this section of the book has unblocked what most people see as a barrier to success.

So, where to go for advice, The places to start are many. Business Links are great, they can link you to the local enterprise agencies, and often have financial counsellors themselves. Banks – yes, bank managers are good starting places, and if nothing else, they can open up other avenues. In fact bank managers are key people when it comes to getting money. Other businesses, and all business people have been faced with similar problems in the past, and most will know of routes you may take. Perhaps people in your family can help. Be open about what you want to do – the more you discuss it the better you will be.

9

The Sales Machine

Why are some people good at selling? Why do some companies never seem to have any problems with getting orders, while others struggle to stay afloat from day to day? It is not that they are better people, or that they are technically better. They are not even luckier – you make your own luck in this world. No, they put the focus where it matters. It is not getting the orders but driving the front end of the sales cycle. It is getting the enquiry, the contacts, the visits or the introductions. The rest will follow. Selling is a numbers game for the new business. The sales are the result of the selling process.

It sounds trite, but I am about to give you a 30-second MBA. It underpins all successful businesses yet, with their complex and fancy ideas, most courses in business studies (that I have come into contact with) seem to assume that you will know this by instinct. Business studies often deal with the peripherals to business, not the essence of your business. My views may outrage academics but it is not meant to devalue what they do, only shine a light on what you must concentrate on and do.

Business is about delighted customers. Hence, the MBA. Easy!

**You give the customers what they want
in a way that delights them, and they are prepared
to pay you the price you ask.**

A 30 second MBA

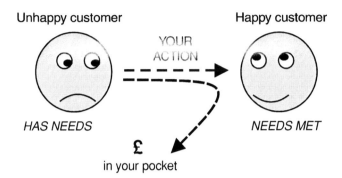

This all seems very simplistic, but it is the essence of what business is all about. Delighted customers are willing to pay what they see as a fair price. Note I did not say a low price. Well, in the vast majority of cases they are – there is always the exception that proves the rule. Let your competitors deal with him! He can be their problem.

So, to round off this academic gem of wisdom, how do you go about making this work? Why try to be clever?

> ### *Ask customers what they want.*

Do not tell them what they need, nor what you can do. Ask them simply *what they want*. Then provide it at a profit. You can charge what the market will stand. Forget the idea of a fair price and low cost. After all, you must make a profit.

Examples are legion. Restaurants, clothes, cars, holidays, clubs, supermarkets – you name it and that seems to be the run of the green! Prices must be set to allow you to make a profit. Did it take 30 seconds to read and understand? Probably not, more like 5 minutes if you read as slowly as I do. But, if you keep going over it, within days it becomes a matter of second nature. The more you say it, the quicker it becomes.

Back to the sales machine

So what is the sales machine? Well, it's simple. It all comes down to the fact that sales are a numbers game. The more people you see, the more people you talk to, the more effort you make, and the more success you will have in selling. Selling must be seen this way. If you want to sell more, drive the front end of the sales process.

Let's look at estate agency – you have to visit so many properties, do so many valuations, and you will get so many houses on your books. Then to sell the property – they estimate that every 10 or so people who visit will result in an offer being made and probably a sale. So, sales staff in estate agencies are given very specific targets based around this. That is why the offices are often staffed by youngsters who don't seem to know what they're doing and have little experience. Estate agents feel that the skill can be superseded.

If they don't get the number of houses on their books they want, then the answer is simple. They will inflate the price they say you can expect – and we all fall for that – and then, when nobody wants to look, they get you to drop it. Quite an objective way to look at it, but it is the way it works. Little skill, just numbers are important, and are watched like a hawk. Watch the numbers and you will not be far wrong.

A Story

A friend of mine, in a similar field to me, tells the story of his depression when, after two years in business, things were not really working out. One evening, walking his dog, he stopped and stared at a bungalow with a long drive with 'his and hers' Mercedes parked outside. Being Tom, he imagined they must have inherited the money or, worse but more likely, robbed someone. After all, there was a recession!

After a few minutes – it might have been ten – the owner came out and asked him what was the matter. "I'm just looking at the cars. Aren't they lovely." To which came the response, "Oh, do you want to buy one, only I'm buying a Rolls Royce in a few weeks. I promised myself one for my 40th, and it's my birthday soon."

This got to my friend, with his troubles. He reacted. "Don't you know there's a recession on?"

"Recession, what recession? I'm doing better than ever. When trade looks difficult, I just make more effort."

The sales machine

It took a few days for the penny to drop for my friend, but drop it did, and he's never looked back. The thing is a numbers game, and the sales machine is just like a funnel into which you feed contacts, a handle you turn like a mincer, and a narrow outlet from which sales come. Feed the machine and come they will.

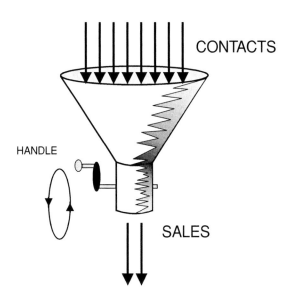

CONTACTS

HANDLE

SALES

The Sales Machine

Let's look at a painter and decorator. Say his first contact with potential customers is when he receives a phone call starting perhaps, "Do you ...?" or "Could you ...?" or "I'm looking for someone to help with ..." or whatever. There follows a conversation. The next stage may involve being asked round for a discussion (no, no job is guaranteed), followed by ideas and a quote. He will try and find a time when he could fit the job in. This is important (most decorators try to overfill their diary with the result that they are planning to upset clients). Then he goes away while the clients make a decision. Will it be him or one of the three others who are all equally able to do the same quality work. All at about the same price!

How can our decorator get more work, expand, or perhaps even take on staff? He could reduce his price, or come up with novel and attractive ideas, the latter of which he should do anyway! By far the most effective way is to see more people, put himself about a bit. Okay, it's not just that, but it is the essential first step. Without this, he is on a hiding to nothing.

Things go in cycles. If he is obviously busy and is pushed for time, then what is the likely effect? These people, with whom he has just invested time, are more likely to pick him simply because, being busy, he must be good. Sod's law.

Advertising and Marketing – what are they?

Where does advertising and marketing come in? What value do they add to the sales effort? The most they can do is to get people 'walking past your shop window', in a manner of speaking. Advertising does not bring you more sales. More people may contact you, but being controversial, I would say that advertising is very hit or miss and leaves a lot to chance. Some is effective; much is a waste of time. And the chances are that the advertising will not live up to your expectations.

Marketing is more useful, but what is marketing? A man who had just passed his marketing exams once told me that I didn't understand marketing, probably because I didn't use his fancy words. But then I had built a successful business. In reality, marketing to me is understanding what people want and just getting your message to the market! Ah, but what message? That depends upon you. No two businesses want to say the same things to the same people. You are trying to influence people's ideas, you want them to want something that you feel only you can provide. So what's so special about you? What are you going to tell them?

How can you 'market' your firm or yourself? What about our decorator? There are more ways than you think. Try some of these creative thoughts – there will be many more.

- Referrals – Ask past satisfied clients who they think you should approach – who would benefit from your work? Get proactive and contact them before they had thought of decorating that lounge!

- Stories in the newspaper – Yes, good old PR, and it needn't cost any money. After all, newspapers are crying out for good copy, especially about local people making good. Without news, nobody buys their paper and they can't sell their advertising! Be creative.

- Leaflets – A neatly designed and printed leaflet can say a great deal about you and your business. Leave a few where likely clients might go. Avoid having them distributed in newspapers, these usually find the bin.

- How about a computer expert running an 'agony aunt' column in the local newspaper – no income but perhaps some good publicity. You may even run surgeries at the village hall. An excellent source of work.

- Concentrate on a few niche skills where you can grow a reputation. Word will spread quickly, helped along of course by you.

- Do something outrageous – one decorator locally advertised himself as 'Bloggs (or whatever) and son and daughter'. From this he got loads of work, because it got him noticed..

The more you think about it, the more ways there are. For sure, watching the television and hoping the phone will ring is perhaps not the best way to gain sales. Shoe leather, telephoning, whatever, there must be ways to put your message across. That's marketing. How are you going to be seen to be different to the rest?

You need to experiment. How many times do I hear people say, "It'll never work." You must experiment to get attention, otherwise you are just like everyone else. Every good idea, every novel approach was just an experiment once. If you are not controversial in business then, you are an also-ran. Sorry.

Being technically able, does this bring you work? Remember that most others in your field are as technically able as you are. Does the larger competitor get to be larger by being more technically able? The chances are no. It is probably not luck either, even though it may look so to you. Remember Pareto's Law? You get 80% of the jobs with 20% of the skill. The answer is **sales**. Selling, putting yourself about, feeding the sales machine, putting yourself through the mincer – that is what it is all about.

Three legged stools

Most people start in business as technicians. "I'm a good plumber, so I'll start a business plumbing." When they are busy, they forget about the sales, they give the accounts to the accountant, and they go forth into the world with a wrench ... or something like that, anyway.

What folly, but the sort of mistakes most people make. Business is like a three-legged stool. The three legs are the doing, the sales and the control of finances. You may not like it but you must be in control of all three. Without that, the stool will fall over. Each leg deserves equal emphasis, even though you may spend more time doing than controlling.

One leg, perhaps the most important, is driving the sales up – without these you don't have a business. The other two are controlling the finances and ... oh yes, doing the work. Make the sales leg strong, because that is the leg you rely on most when times get tough.

Yes, I hear some of you say, I've got one really large customer, and I work 100% of the time for him. When the time comes, you are expendable, and when the time comes, your stool just falls over. Recently, one local manufacturer complained to me that it was unfair that a major client had taken on a new buyer who, at a stroke, had cancelled 30+% of his business, and for no reason. What had happened to his stool?

Yes, there is help in the area of finances, and a good accountant will do much more than just keep your books for you – he will help you get control. But at a cost! The financial side is not really that complicated and just keeping an eye on major figures is often enough – things like income, major costs and profit (which is that bit left over when you've paid yourself, remember?).

But where is the help getting sales? Who else but you will get you work, and if you employ a salesperson, how do you know he or she is doing enough?

Most small businesses have the endless problem of finding work when they are busy doing. That takes discipline. You can't be selling when you're doing, and you can't be doing when you're selling. And you're not big enough to afford a full time salesperson. The thing about doing the work is that it brings in the money, and is often more fun than selling, after all. So it's easy to see why sales get forgotten. You must feed the sales machine, and this takes time. You must allow time for marketing now to overcome future famine. If it means time must be better managed – then manage your time. Ask others where you could be better!

Do not control what comes out of the sales machine, drive what goes in. You must push the front end of the business, and if that gives you the operational problems of being too busy, then there are easier problems to deal with than not enough work! Like the estate agency, they control the numbers they need to feed their machine. They control visits, estimates, and houses taken on, visits and of course sales. The rest is of no consequence. And if one house stays on their books for ages, so what?

How important is price, really?

People continually tell me that it's tough out there and customers want the lowest price. I agree that nobody wants to pay more than they feel they have to, but all too often price cuts are an easy way out, just there to 'buy' work. And just because the visible price is apparently low, it doesn't mean you charge a low price.

Sometimes though it is important to be creative with price so that you can both appear low cost and can make stacks of profit. It's being seen to offer price advantage. Supermarkets are past masters at this, they have it down to a fine art. Some lines have a known value – known value items – and these are competitive But most do not, and here supermarkets make a killing. Of the many thousand of lines on offer only a dozen or so are known. The supermarket's argument is that they add value to the goods. But to increase the price by 400% just to wash and bag lettuce? Be like the supermarkets. Price things creatively.

We love the British!

When you are selling, there are two basic kinds of people. There are the traditional British, and the rest of the world. There is something unusual about the make-up of the British, and they have several traits it is important to remember when selling, and I'll mention a few here.

● *The British love problems.* That is probably the reason why soaps are so popular! They are less likely to buy a dream as they are a solution to a problem. If you are seen to understand the problem first, there will be a lot of empathy between you and customer. It's not everyone, but probably 75% of the population are this way. Link the benefits you bring to the types of problems customers may encounter and you will have a better chance of success. And if our decorator wants to improve his service, then addressing these problems is a good starting point.

● *The British are a cynical lot.* It does not pay to give too many benefits, or say too much because, in the majority of cases, you are just giving them a reason NOT to buy. It sounds crazy, but it's true. Know the value of knowing what not to say, and keep some benefits up your sleeve for later.

● Everyone loves to talk, and the best salesmen know when to shut up. More true of the British than many, the salesperson who says nothing is felt to understand the problems, to know what the customer feels and to be totally at one with the customer. The customers sell themselves.

Your own personal thermometer!

Most of us work to our own internal thermostat, and the sales machine is usually set to this. If we are not earning enough, then we make greater effort, but when we approach the top of the scale, our efforts seem to slow down and we almost relax and stop. If you are starting in business, you need to adopt a different view of money, almost take a 'monopoly money' approach. Otherwise your sales effort will be doomed to failure. To replicate a salary or wage, when you're working for yourself, you need to aim for double that as money coming to the business. Don't forget that when you are on holiday or out selling you are not earning.

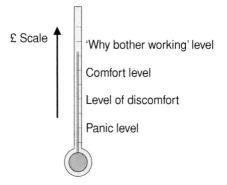

Personal earnings thermometer

Where your levels are set depends upon you. If you are comfortable on an income of £10,000 per annum, then when your income nears that level, your effort level will reduce. It is your inbuilt thermostat if you like, that stops you working when you don't need to.

But you set the level. This thermostat can be adjusted, albeit slowly. If you were operating at a turnover of, say, £50,000, then it would not be unreasonable to set your heights at say £55,000 or

£60,000. Perhaps to leap to £1 million is a bit aggressive (but if you can, then great). Numbers are all relative, and as long as you think it is achievable, your target must be realistic.

Taking orders and selling

There is a big difference between taking orders and selling. I see it all around, especially in shops where I would have thought it less than likely. Selling is absolutely vital, but unfortunately is an underestimated skill. There is a vast difference between taking someone's order and actually selling to them! Just because you are called a sales assistant, and take money, it doesn't mean you are actually selling anything. Most don't, they wait until the customer approaches and says, "I wish to buy this."

Let's look at a typical scenario. Into the shop you go, armed with an amount of money and a determination to get what you feel you want. You go to the counter, ask for a bag of biscuits (for example), pay your money and go. Have they sold you anything? No. They have taken your order, met your minimum expectations and that is all. Have they sold you any cakes, or more biscuits, or a loaf of bread, or even an idea that you may come in more often? Have you walked out with more than you intended to buy when you walked in? No. So they have not sold you anything.

Consider supermarkets. Go in for biscuits and you are likely to walk out with a whole bag of groceries. My wife forbids me to go shopping alone because I spend too much. Yes, we are all caught. Why? Because they actually sell. Everything in a supermarket is geared to sales. From where things are positioned to colours, aromas, makes, and signs – the arena of selling in supermarkets is approached as a science! They are good at it! Even so, it is unlikely that an assistant will approach you and try to sell you anything – you are lured into being sold to by the supermarket's cleverness.

What value jargon?

Here is a bit of marketing jargon. Sorry. Classic marketing talks about the 4 Ps – Product, Price, Position and Promotion. You must have the right product, at the right price, position it correctly in the marketplace and promote it the right way. Yes, if you are Mr Unilever of Mr Marks and Spencer. But not so for Mr Average. The same rules just don't hold true to the same degree. Builders have their own variation of the 4 Ps, position, position, position and position. These drive the price, and so it is for you.

Position yourself and your product/service correctly and the others fall naturally into place. It then becomes common sense that you try not to sell the wrong thing to the wrong person. Back to the MBA – if you are selling what the client wants, there is no problem.

Back to price

What stems from this is the issue of price as a key to selling. It is not the key. That is a fallacy. It is an excuse for not selling, or not having to sell. Let us be cynical again. If you employ a salesperson, what's the easiest thing for him or her to do? Excuses can be made for poor sales skills by saying that the price is too high or the competition is too fierce. Any purchaser will try to squeeze price, and will ask for better. That is only natural. The temptation for the salesperson is then to 'give away' the sale at the lowest price possible. It was none other than the easy option with a ready made excuse that you can't check up on.

But what if it's you that's facing this? It is the natural trap when you negotiate on price. Be more creative and link price to service levels. "If you want me to lower the price, I can do that. But then that will adversely impact ..." Be open and say that you price it fairly, and others will cut corners if they charge less than you! Yes, price sensitivity is an excuse, as long as you are in the same ballpark. If you are willing to lower price once, anybody in their right mind will expect similar or better discounts next time!

If price were the main issue when it comes to buying, we'd all be driving cars at the cheapest end of the market. Who would go for a Rolls Royce, or a Jaguar, or a Mercedes, or whatever? The chances are that, although Ladas may be very good cars, and may well improve further in image in the future, there are a number of criteria that come into play. These are:

- Image — people who have money spend it
- Reliability — what good is a cheap product that keeps breaking?
- Status — much like image but more refined. Who is important?
- Value — this could give options, backup, or the impact it will have
- Fashion — ask any woman the importance of fashion
- Comfort — the cost of cheap clothes for example is discomfort.

And there are many more ...

So, stay away from price as a major issue, do not make it more important than it really is.

Pigeon holes

Customers do tend to associate suppliers with a limited range of goods, and put you in pigeonholes. What does this mean for you and your sales effort? It means there is a massive opportunity for you that remains untapped. Your sales machine could be well fed by this alone!

Look at your customers afresh. How can you set about breaking the mould? Ask the following questions (obviously be a bit sensitive otherwise it may impact the wrong way).

- "How can I help you further?"
- "What other services do you need?"
- "What kind of problems do you have with others? "

What about complaints and stuff

How effective are you at supporting your sales machine, or do you make it hard work? Do you shoot yourself in the foot? How well do you live up to promises?

Only one customer in twenty-five complains direct to your face. The rest rubbish you to others and go elsewhere, telling a dozen or so friends along the way. A delighted customer will tell ten other people, an unhappy customer will tell twenty-four, so it's in your interest not to have people complain – bad marketing or what?

So, for every complaint, you are likely to have a bad name with many dozens of potential customers. For every delighted customer probably there will probably be another not quite so large group who have heard well of you. Not fair perhaps because the odds are stacked against you but it does show that excellent work does have a positive effect and, if you slip, the consequences can be dire. This is not to put you off, more to make you see potential and consequences.

Tips

There are several other issues that may help drive your sales machine. We've already mentioned briefly the importance of referrals. Insurance salesmen use this technique all the time. And it works because you would not be given a lead considered cold. Already, you have had your leads screened by the giver, and these leads will be half sold with the value of a reference. There are other tips that may help:

- *Anecdotes & stories.* Insurance salesmen have all got a sob story of someone who had failed to buy insurance and in every industry and trade, there is opportunity to use the idea to advantage. It adds weight to what you say.

- *Psychology of numbers.* The number 7 is good. Try to understand the value that certain things bring – almost psychologically. You may not understand nor agree with the theory, but if it has an impact then why not try it.

- *Don't give too much choice.* A simple alternative will do, and in choosing, they are already a long way towards buying. To say no then becomes so much harder.
  ? "Do you want black or green?"
  ? "Would you like me to deliver, or will you collect?"
  ? "I'm visiting the area soon. Would you prefer this week or next?"
  And so on ... there are endless variations.

- *Use 'tie downs'.* These are simple re-affirmations after a statement to get assent. For example:
  ! "These do fit well, don't they!"
  ! "This type of service is better for your company, isn't it!"
  ! "You do feel I have understood the issues, don't you?"

  There are all manner of variations again on this, but with these tie downs, you are also gaining small agreements which are all steps along the road to getting a sale.

- *Feeling good.* There is a strong relationship between how good we feel, and how well we sell. So, always be good to yourself and stay fit, dress reasonably well, and do not let work be the only focus of your life – otherwise you will not enjoy the benefits of hard work.

Many people try to tell me that it is important to increase sales. But when it comes down to it, all they can do is complain when fancy techniques on how to close sales or improve their techniques don't work. When it comes to the crunch, sales are vital to the success of all businesses, but newer companies are especially vulnerable, mainly because the person who starts is not a salesman – or not a good one anyway. Yet.

Success will not depend upon techniques, it depends upon where you place the emphasis. If you need sales, understand the sales cycle and put the emphasis where it counts – right at the very beginning. I will never try to make you a salesperson, but I aim to make you more effective at getting work!

10

How Much Should I Charge?

Wherever I go, people tell me about competition, tough times, cheap imports and lack of money. And many use this as a driving reason why their prices must be held down, almost to the point where not only do they not make a profit, they don't even make a living. Why then are they in business?

It's easy to say, but a simple rule of thumb is that if you can't make a profit doing what you're doing, you shouldn't be doing it. You should be doing something else. Profit all boils down to a few simple things, all of which are interconnected. These revolve around three core issues:

1. **how much you do**
2. **how much you charge for doing it**
3. **what your costs are.**

All are very closely linked. How much you do will be influenced by how much you charge, but I am going to stick to the principle in this book that I would rather do less but better, and charge more for it. I would rather work smart than work hard for no return. Yes, I agree, times may change but, in all honesty, they don't look to be on the move yet – and you could wait a long time. So, a motto:

Work smart, not hard

Just to re-emphasise. There is little point in trying to get bigger if, at the end of the day, all you get is more work and no reward. Your efforts must be rewarded, and rewarded well. Without that, there is no point in being in business. Few people go into business as a charitable venture. I know one or two, but for them business is an interest and not otherwise important. Sadly, I am not in the same fortunate position. It would be nice, but I'm not there yet.

When pricing your goods, please remember this – you are in business to make money. Price accordingly. If you make a profit and you grow, and then you make more profit, fine. If you cut price to grow, or do not charge enough in the first place, then you are on a hiding to nothing.

The influence of price.

Price influences everything – from the way your product is seen in relation to competition, to the volume of sales, the amount of service you can give to customers, the profit you make, the wages you take, the quality of life, the motivation of staff and your own self esteem. That and much more, what you charge touches everything. The price of what you do is central to your business. It requires thought. It all boils down to really how you see yourself, and what do you want for your business and family.

Price not only affects the way you see yourself, it also affects the way others see you. If you offer low prices, people assume you work to lower standards, lower quality, and therefore your product is not as good. That's life. This will not stop them complaining if your widget breaks down – they probably expected it to in the first place.

Profit is dirty word, and few people want to actively help you make it, but everyone realises that when you are in business, to stay in business, you need to make a profit. You must price accordingly.

It is not as easy as that. You cannot charge the earth and provide poor service. It is a balancing act, but perhaps it is best described by a comparison of two garages where you might have your car fixed. These typical examples are to be found everywhere.

🚗 One will do all sorts of work for you at no extra charge. Nice guy, always smiles, but his business is the same as it has been for years. Never any investment, always struggles to make ends meet. You go to his garage for the basic work because you know he will do a few extra odds and sods. You can always get the car booked in. Also, he will never run up a big bill, he knows you'd complain if he did.

🚗 On the other hand there is the other garage, probably a main dealer, costs the earth, always busy, lots of equipment. You go to this garage when you want an important job done, and while you are there will have a few irritating problems sorted as well. Always there is a big bill, but you expect that and don't complain. Only one problem, he's so busy you can't get your car booked in for weeks.

There's a message in this, and it isn't too hard to see. If you were the garage owner, which would you rather be? Which would you rather was your garage?

Do not undervalue yourself.

Remember that profit is what is left after you have paid yourself. So you have to cover your costs, buy your materials, pay yourself and still make a profit. Don't forget this when you are setting your prices. It is only too easy to forget the profit element, or confuse yourself into thinking that the profit element is what you pay yourself.

Many people undervalue their efforts, and sell themselves short. Why are you worth less than Bloggs and Co. down the road? In your eyes, you should be worth more. You own your own company and you have taken responsibility for your own destiny, whereas Bloggs and Co. employ people who have less commitment than you – both to the business and the customers.

You need to reinforce the idea of value, both in your own and your customers' minds. To do so takes the mind off cost. It is one thing to sell a widget, quite another to consider the value you add to it. You must therefore build the value you add into the price you charge.

There is no such thing as a free lunch, remember. Take a shopkeeper in a corner shop. Yes, they sell items you find in supermarkets and discount stores. How can they re-inforce the idea of value, how can they start to value themselves well? I would like to relate a story told to me recently:

> Some years ago a businessman was forced from his country and came to Britain with virtually nothing, just a few hundred pounds and the clothes he had on, together with his family. He had to make a living. So he leased a shop, and opened for business. There was not much in the shop, but it was clean. You could have eaten from the floors it was so clean. When asked for something he didn't have, he apologised and said, "Sorry, but if you are going to be a regular customer, I will stock it for you." Market research as he was going along! His shop got busier and busier.
>
> He had noticed one key point. Unlike some countries, here there is no such thing as a fixed price. So our friend recognised that he could charge a premium and make a good profit. So, where is the value that he adds?
>
> Well, already we know that his customers know he will be stocking the things they want. When they said it would be good to open later, he did just that. When they wanted earlier opening, he did that too. Everything was tailored to his customer's needs. But he did charge a premium. He was not cheap. Why should he be? He was providing a service, and it was the service customers valued, not the cost of the item they needed. Even knowing he was expensive, they still shopped. Now he has a chain of smaller, local supermarkets around the West Midlands. He has 'made it'.

My own experience is similar. My company provided what I thought was excellent value, but admittedly the unit price was higher than for similar products sold down the road. Occasionally people would ask me to lower prices to compete. I would go the other way. "If you want to try theirs, I wish you all the best. Give them a try, and I'll see you in a few weeks when you realise there's more to life than price." Without exception I would see them again within a few days.

If you value yourself, give quality service, then people (when they have sampled quality) will be unwilling to return to what they see as a poorer substitute.

Find out what your customers want ... provide it at a profit.

Remember the MBA? When it comes to pricing, then the MBA is essential. What do customers want? Our friend with the small supermarkets realised, as do I, that what customers want is more than the product they have come to buy. He recognised the need for cleanliness and service with flexible and long opening hours.

With my business, customers wanted a perception of quality, choice, fresh produce and hygienic service, friendly staff, convenience, personal service ... as well as the many other ingredients that made our business work well.

Identify what it is your customers want. They need the item or service they are buying, but they will want it provided in particular ways that reflect the way they are or the way they do business. It is the *provision* of the needs, in *the way they want* it, which takes the focus off price and let's you charge a more realistic amount. Give customers what they want and charge for it.

What should you charge?

What you should really charge is simple. Charge what the market will stand, as long as that makes you a profit. We live in a free market. You can see market pricing all around you. The raw ingredients of meals cost around the same, wherever you go.

Why then are some restaurants able to charge huge amounts of money for small portions and in the café round the corner you can get a plateful for a couple of quid!

The world of fashion is similar. A piece of cloth in some shops sells for many thousand of pounds when it has a designer label on it. A very similar item coming in from the Far East sells for £5 on the local market. Where is the difference in value? Well – it must be in the mind of the beholder.

These are examples but they serve to emphasise the point. You can charge what the market will stand, not some idea of a fair price. Fair is a relative word. Do not be ashamed of thinking yourself and your product (or service) as being of high value.

The value of reputation

Oh, I understand, you are just starting in business and feel that you do not have the right to demand higher prices. You could be right, and if you feel that way, you are right. But then, you could be doing what most people do, you could be undervaluing yourself again.

What value is reputation. How do good reputations come about? You may have your name in the paper, but all you have to do is tell the newspapers you're great and they will go round telling everybody else how good you are. You could be referred, but most referrals come because you have asked for one, so that's not too hard.

Other than that your reputation is what you tell your potential customer about yourself. If you say you have a good reputation, then as far as the potential customer is concerned, you've got one until you mess up!

The oddity here is the high street, in seemingly terminal decline in this country anyway. Here, you can have a good reputation that is seriously enhanced by the fact that you've been there longer than anyone else – survived better than many others. It really says nothing about you, but you can destroy this fragile existence and rosy reputation quite easily. So, where you have a shop front, you do need to be a touch more careful.

So what is the value of reputation? If you say you have a good reputation, then you have – as long as you do not 'screw up' as the phrase goes. Your reputation is therefore valued at what you say it is – and you build it into your price accordingly. Why hide your light under a bushel. If you want people to think you're good, put your price up!

Volume / Price trade-off

There is always going to be a trade-off between volume and price. As your price increases, so fewer people will either want or be able to pay for your services. This is normal. Do not feel that you have to reach, nor sell to everyone – target your market. You should not want to do business with everybody. You probably couldn't anyway. That way you become a busy fool.

Remember the sums. Your costs stay the same (approximately) or can even go up as volume of turnover increases. If your price comes down even a little, then volume has to increase substantially to even maintain current profit levels.

As an example, let's say John sells his widgets at £10 each. With a Gross Profit of 10%, he makes £1 clear profit on each widget (net profit before tax etc) after he's paid everything, even himself. Say he cuts his price by a mere 5% because he has a manic idea that his widgets are too expensive, or because someone tells him he's too dear, or because a competitor has cut his price. His costs stay the same at first, so he now only makes 50p per widget. He will have to double sales to keep profit levels up to past levels.

Then come the hidden problems. Because he wants twice as many widgets, he cannot get credit and needs to borrow from the bank. Interest and other charges put more pressure on profit. He has to employ more salesmen who are not yet experienced. These people need cars, which require up-front costs – more pressure on the bank. And so it goes on, John has seen profit eliminated simply by reducing his price by a small amount to increase turnover. Oh, and what has happened to turnover? Well, local competitors have all reduced their prices to stay competitive. So John's stocks have gone up, costs have gone up, staff have gone up, temperature's gone up, and the only thing to go down has been profit.

So in this trade-off between price and volume, you must remember one issue – Profit. It is well to be busy, but not to be a busy fool. Remember as well the old adage:

Turnover is vanity, profit is sanity.

The Pricing Matrix

The more complicated the business gets then, for the average smaller business, the less that detailed management tools will be used. There is one simple tool that will help enormously in setting prices. This is not a 'one off' exercise, and must be done and kept up on a regular basis. Not a great lover of being too formal, this is the one tool that stands out from the rest.

This important tool is the Pricing Matrix. Let me give you an example of how it works. Like many things, it is effective because it is very easy. You simply list out your competitors down one side of a matrix, put their products and services on another side, the fill in the matrix with the prices. Oh yes, what is a matrix – it is simply a piece of paper ruled into squares, however big you want these squares to be. Complicated? Sounds it perhaps, but let's see it working. You will see that it is very easy.

We know we have five competitors, companies A, B, C, D and E. None do exactly the same as we do, but all operate in the same kind of area. There are 4 basic product types numbered 1 to 4 for convenience. It should not be beyond the wit of man to find out how much each charges for each product group. This is simple for products but can be just as effective when dealing with quite complex services. The secret of the matrix is to keep it simple, so that you can not only understand it but also describe what you are doing to a friend. It makes no difference how many products or how many competitors, that just makes the matrix bigger and it takes longer to do.

Competitor	Product 1	Product 2	Product 3	Product 4
Competitor A	£2.50		£3.75	
Competitor B	£4.00	£6.00	£3.50	
Competitor C		£7.10	£2.90	£6.75
Competitor D	£5.50			£5.50
Competitor E		£5.00	£1.90	

From the matrix, we can compare prices for comparable products and services from all our local competitors. It is not too difficult, and at times there will seem to be logic, and at other times it will seem totally illogical. Do not try to be too detailed, it is only a guide at present. Without this kind of information, you are flying blind in business!

One thing you will begin to notice from this is that prices will either all be about the same for a product, in which case you can't be too far away, or they will be all over the place. Chances are the latter. Think back to when you last wanted a quote, or went to buy a service, whatever it may be. Prices are seldom too similar, unless they have been fixed! So having done your research, how much should you charge? Do not try to be cheap. Do not try to be average. Try to make some real money. Be in the upper quartile across the board.

The Upper Quartile!

What, you may ask, is a quartile? Well, the upper quartile is that area between ¾ and the top on any scale. So the area you should be looking to aim for with your prices is not the top, because that makes you look expensive (unless you are obviously the best, and somebody has to be both best and most expensive). Aim to be not too far from the top.

In the example above, what sort of prices could you ask? I would suggest you should price Product 1 around £5, Product 2 around £6.50, Product 3 around £3.50 and Product 4 around the £6.50 mark. All seem pretty reasonable, without giving it too much thought. You alone will know whether you are able to put your service out at that price at a profit. It makes no difference how big, how small, how many this, how much that. It is all about your own belief that justifies the price you charge. Price is a relative thing.

Ah, I hear you say, but what makes mine worth that much more? Easy! It's the additional service you add to justify the price. And to understand just what that means, you need to know what your customer wants, as well as where your competitors are falling down. You may be lucky, have supreme confidence, but unless you want to take a chance, give the service.

The nice thing about setting your prices high is that you can always bring your prices down if you set them too high, but it's a bugger to get them up if you start too low. To me, the caution is on the high side, not the low. But then I look at business as trying to make money by selling what you are trying to do, not doing something then trying to sell it.

That is only a guide. Remember that price is determined by supply and demand. I will repeat for you another short story that has stayed with me ever since the first time I heard it. It sums up the idea of price and value in everyday language, in words that everybody relates to. It is called the Parable of the Ford Escort.

The Parable of the Ford Escort

One day a man decided to fix the left backlight of his wife's Ford Escort. The price asked for a replacement unit by the local Ford dealership, for a new light unit was ... a lot of money. We've all had to buy that simple part which, with a captive market, we feel is a rip off. So taking life in both hands, almost like stepping into alien territory, this man decided to go to a local scrap merchant. Actually, there were about 5 car breakers close together, so he was confident that he would get what he wanted there.

At the first of these breakers he asked how much the light

was. "Oh, they're £10, but we haven't got one to fit that model – try Charlie's down the road." Thanking him for his help, he went to Charlie's where he got much the same response. "Oh, they're £10, but we haven't got one to fit that model, try next door." The story was the same at the other three yards as well. £10 each, but nobody had one.

Disappointed, he was resigned to buying a new fitting when he remembered Yellow Pages. There he found a car breaker, quite local, who specialised in Fords. He rang them up and, yes, they had the part. "Put one by for me, I'll be on my way in 5 minutes."

On arriving, he went straight to the counter and asked for the bit which was handed to him, all clean and tidy. "That'll be £15 please," said the man behind the counter.

"£15 – that's a bit dear!" said our friend who had been told a consistent £10 by every other car breaker. "Every other scrap man said the price was only £10." So the man behind the counter asked where he had been, whom he had seen and what had been said.

"Did they have one to sell to you?" the man behind the counter finally asked.

"No," our friend admitted.

"Then I'll tell you. When I haven't got one, the price will be £10, but today I have got one, and the price to you is £15. If you want, you can go to the dealer and buy a new one."

The Parable of the Ford Escort. Hidden in there are some very important messages that you would do well to ponder. Rather than give you my thoughts, see how many core messages you can get out of what is quite simply an example of real street life. List them down.

There are many elements of good business sense in what others say is just being street wise!

No 7 is not just a bus route

Certain numbers have significance. The number 13 is thought by many to be unlucky, and the number 9 is thought to have mystical qualities. The number 7 is also considered by many to have some mystical benefits.

As a number, 7 is about average. Not high nor low, the number 7 seems to be a number which people are very comfortable with. I have heard it said often that a price tag with the number 7 in it would induce people to buy, will actually encourage people to part with money.

I don't know if this is true or not, but I have always found it helpful in hindsight. It may work for you, it may not, but you may at least want to try it. It may be that the price you ask is £7 instead of £6.80, or similar. Who knows, it may be just the thing you are looking for.

People are strange. 'There's nowt so strange as folk' is a northern expression and very true. We have some strange ways that almost defy explanation. Do not fight them – in fact, use them for all they're worth.

Look for other little things that help people buy. Colour, scent, packaging, display – you may ignore them yourself, but in business you ignore them at your peril. If, when you are deciding prices, you get even a small advantage from using numbers creatively, then why not try?

Price rises – how do you go about them?

When you face your customers, the last things you want to wave at them are price rises. Lowering prices is always easier. Price rises are never popular. Who wants to give more money for something they have a real need for and have been using for a while. It always gets a moan, well nearly always. But you can make it less difficult and even use it as an aid to improving sales. But how?

Start by putting your prices up in writing. If you do not, then people will not believe you and this will result in arguments and bad feeling. So, make a big, clear notice:

> ## As of 1st April, prices will go up by 4.5%.

So everyone now knows that from the 1st April, prices will go up. How can that be seen positively? Just add another sentence that offers some encouragement towards acceptance:

> **We will hold down prices
> to that date.**

What happens? It encourages sales at the old price as people buy up old stock (this releases cash to you and shifts stock). Second, it encourages bulk purchases, and third, it means that, when the time comes, the price rise just seems to slip into place.

Discounts.

Discounts have been discussed elsewhere. For me, they are just an invitation to give away your profits. However, if there are traditions in your industry to give discounts, then build them into your prices right from the start.

A good example of this is the occasional trend to run with large 'sales' on through an industry. It takes a brave person to step outside this trend. People love a bargain, and this trend caters to that love, but please be careful, as you can really get confused on prices, and you can easily run foul of legislation, especially if you are trying to compete with the national chains.

Dress prices up, and use the word 'Only'

Price itself is a number. Of concern to the purchaser is how that number relates to the product or service, and how it is described. There are some very powerful words that can go with a price, which have the effect of making a number seem much smaller than it actually is. One of these words, in common use by many larger companies, is the word 'only'.

If you ask £10 for an item, it has a price which may be considered high and it does not show 'value'. If you ask 'Only £10', it is a relative price, and that price has been judged to be relatively low, and be good value. It matters not that it is you who have been the judge. You have

114

already started to influence the buyer in their choice of who should supply them with what they need. You have already transmitted value into the word, and given an element of worth. Oh yes, it is a very subtle suggestion, a blatant use of a word, but it does work, time and again.

There will be other words and phrases that have the same or a similar effect. Phrases such as 'price promise', 'value', 'cut the cost', 'you can't buy better', 'price freeze', and the good old 'If you can buy the same cheaper locally we will refund the difference'. All of these are designed to make you as the customer feel that you are spending money wisely. The last of these phrases always amuses me, mainly because these offers are commonly offered on models and packages which are only supplied by one supplier, so can't be found elsewhere. Anything similar from elsewhere may look the same to the naked eye, but there will be a difference.

When it all boils down to it, the issue of selling is all a game and everyone plays it for all they are worth. Yes, I know many people feel that this is not part of being in business, but it is. You just have to develop your own style and use words and phrases that suit you. That way, you feel less embarrassed, but it important that you get the right emphasis and priorities.

But what if Price is key?

If price is absolutely vital, for example in a tendering situation (where you are giving a sealed price for certain services), then you do have to be a bit sharper. If price is such a major issue then you have got to be sharp. And the only way you can be that is to look very carefully at what is needed, provide just what is asked, and cut your costs.

So how can you make profit? You need to be creative and look for opportunity. Make variations on how you package things. You wanted this, now you want that – that will cost you £x. Obviously if you are tendering, then experience will tell you that there are likely to be areas where differences will occur, and these are the areas to look for. This is where you really stand to make some money – or get somebody out of deep mire so they owe you lots of favours and more profitable jobs elsewhere.

"Oh no, that doesn't happen," I hear you say. Of course not, but just ask yourself how some companies get to do so much work for one particular customer in the first place. I can name companies, big and small, where this is very likely a major issue – it goes on everywhere. Use it to your advantage.

Of course I can say that when you have a good relationship with an existing customer, one you do much work for, this is less the case. You need to be more thoughtful, less grasping. You need to show you are not greedy. By that, you will develop a more co-operative attitude all round, and win more work as a result.

Known Value Items

A similar kind of trick, used more in retailing, is that of 'known value items'. These are, and must be, competitive, simply because everyone knows the sort of price to expect. The 'typical shopping basket' is a good example of this. Some products have a known value, and these are at the forefront of the decision maker's mind when deciding where to shop.

It's the other things you are talked into buying where the supplier profits. Ask yourself, of the items in your shopping bag, which prices do you know, even within 5%. Chances are that it's very few. You accept prices at face value.

You could keep certain prices down, but make profits on associated lines. It is then down to you to be creative in the way you describe and sell these high price lines, and the way you package the product or service to enable you to do that.

Perhaps it is being cynical, but most large retailers have got big, well known and profitable by being cynical. What matters at the end of the day is the profit on the value you add. That comes from two things, the price you charge and the costs you pay. If you are limited at one end by how much the market will stand, then you must look for alternative supplies.

There are a number of simple options, which few people actually grasp. They assume that these routes are not really open.

● *Find alternative, cheaper suppliers.* This may involve using a slightly different or lower specification, or just shopping around. Some wallpapers are cheaper from stockists than to buy direct from the manufacturer. The same is also true of other things. Do not assume you are automatically getting the best deal from a manufacturer.

- *Speak to your suppliers.* Tell them their prices are making you uncompetitive, and that without some movement on price, you will have to shop elsewhere. If you are finding this, then so will all other people who buy from them.

- Look at other ways of *cutting your costs.*

- *Find other services* you can add to the package so that the costs you incur are spread over more jobs, and effectively are reduced in proportion. Look at any industry and you will see this happening.

Pricing therefore comes full circle. It is not an exact science, as many would have you believe. I went through a ritual of deciding prices when in business, but when the truth be known, we put up prices by what we believed the market would stand. To be fair on us, we didn't made high margins on everything, but the science involved with pricing really is minimal. Pricing is more an art than science.

Pricing is an art

Pricing is down to knowing your customers, what they want and what you feel you can get them to pay. It is nothing more than that. That and your confidence at making your prices stick. To do that there will be times when you will have to walk away from jobs that you could get with just a reduction in your price. It all comes down to confidence. Obviously the more people you see, the more people will be inclined to buy from you at a higher price, providing you are targeting the right people. There is no point in trying to sell a high priced service in a poorer area. You will have lots of people who want, but few that can afford to buy.

Equally valid is the need to show common sense. Your whole package may have other flaws than high price. It is easy to blame the price for the problem of not being able to sell. I acknowledge though that there are national and local guides for price, whether for product groups or industries, which do need to be recognised. These may superimpose their guidance upon you, even though you think them wrong. You then need creativity. But if your 'stuff' is not selling, one of the problems may be (but it's not the first thing to look at) a price set too high relative to the way your customer sees what they are getting.

And yes, back to the Pricing Matrix – always keep that going, because you can be assured that your customers will know what your competitors are charging. So you had better know too!

11

Staff – The Hardest Part of Being in Business

The title reflects the views of many that being in business would be easy if it wasn't for staff. That is not really fair, because when questioned closer, many business people are very complimentary about the majority of their people. It's just that the bad apples really stand out from the crowd. They're the ones that cause you grief.

Back to the Pareto principle, you will get 80% of your staff problems from 20% of the people. The object of this chapter is to improve the odds in your favour. You will still get problems, but they will not be threatening to the very existence of your business, as it struggles to grow.

Various groups have devoted much time to studying the area of recruiting and keeping staff, and much work has decided that which we all know to be true. Correct choice of staff has a huge impact on productivity, in terms of monetary gains as well as in the quantity and quality of the service you provide. The trouble is, getting and motivating staff isn't easy, and most new employers often get it wrong, to their cost.

Getting it wrong means incompetent staff, high turnover and problems with unfair dismissal and bad working relationships. The whole business gets dragged down and costs you dear in time, money, frustration and stress. New businesses as well as long established firms have little chance of recouping the cost.

If it works well, recruitment is great. However, few of us are naturally skilled at picking the right people. It is often therefore like a game of chance. In my view, like love and marriage, there is not one right person, but there are many good people out there. The secret is looking to meet the right sort of person. Then, for the relationship to flourish, you both have to work at it.

Most people problems arise because of a conflict of attitude. When was the last time you heard of a person being sacked for being unable to do the job technically? It does happen, but more often than not, I come across firms only too willing to retain good people whose skills have lagged behind technology.

For you, as any employer, the purpose of recruitment is to obtain the right number and quality of people to operate your business to peak performance – at minimum cost. It does not mean employing friends and family, friends of a friend, pretty girls, the first to apply, the cheapest or the closest. It does not mean taking on someone you instantly like, even though that makes you feel good at the time. It does mean being a bit hard-nosed, waiting and getting the right kind of person, even if the skill match is not quite right.

There are lots of traps that you must be aware of. If not, you will be as frustrated as the majority of employers who see staff as a necessary evil in operating their businesses. Would you believe, employees often see employers in the same light – a necessary evil – in some cases? Didn't you? A salutary lesson learned once and never forgotten is that, as employer, the onus is on you to make it work. It is down to you to pick the best, take the lead to get the best out of staff, and that must start with getting the right kind of person, and going about getting people in a way that helps everyone to come out smiling.

Business Needs

The first and most essential question to ask is what the business needs, not what you fancy. Does the vacancy really exist, if so is it one full-time, or several part-timers. It comes back to the business plan again – sorry to be a bore, but that one document is central to so many things. Without this, employing someone (quite a responsibility) could be just a knee-jerk reaction to a problem, perhaps one of your own making.

Despite recent changes in labour law, all of which seems to make employment more expensive and harder to get out of, you do have some flexibility. It is worth speaking to someone like the Enterprise Agency or your local Business Link and seeing if they can get you some free advice. There are some excellent free booklets available, if you just ask. Other than this, you really should be very thoughtful as to what you need. I hope some of the 'thoughts' to follow will help.

Background issues

It needs to be said, early on, that employing people is something that requires thought. The things you want will vary from job to job, industry to industry, and between individual employers, and what you need to do is think about the kind of person you want on board. Some of the vital factors that you ought to consider would be:

👫 *Background* – do you want someone whose background is around maintaining systems, say, in quality, admin or accounts; or would a bureaucratic background be seen as a possible liability where you need someone who is easy outside of structure? Is there a personality issue?

👫 Are there *age limits* or preferred age groups. For the military, you are positively over the hill at 40, (unless you're a general or something), but in some areas, especially in business, the experience that age brings can have value.

👫 *Mobility* – the need for a driving licence is one thing, but to ask a person to move home can be a touch less easy, unless you can absolutely show it to be essential, and in that case make it known very early on – perhaps in any advert.

👫 *Sex, the great divide, and other discrimination.* Seldom is there such an emotive area as discrimination. New employers fall prey to legislation almost at the drop of a hat. You just don't consider you are causing problems and then there you are in court. All I can say here is, be careful, and take advice. Just be careful.

Just a note on discrimination – I personally feel that, if you discriminate, the loser in the longer term will be you. In my experience I have found that those discriminated against often turn out to have many hidden advantages, often because we spend too much time looking for the wrong attributes. To me, the idea of race, sex or background is irrelevant unless it has a specific bearing on the role being considered.

Define the requirements of the job

The trouble is, many jobs are created as a knee-jerk reaction to an immediate problem. Most small business people who interview prospective staff think only of the moment. They do not naturally think whether they can do things in a different way – which means not having to employ. Equally, few think that it is cheaper to buy in services. An example here is payroll – often a payroll clerk is employed when it could be done more cheaply and better by using an agency.

It is devastating to know that often a job description has been drawn up dependent upon how the interviewer or boss would do the job, even when they are not really qualified. Thus skill needs are often described in narrow and restrictive terms. The nice thing about technology is that some traditional skills are becoming less important as technology takes over. But, like before, we are losing balance, and now experience is being ignored, simply because older people are not often so comfortable with computers. As an employer, you would be advised to maintain balance.

One way to build a solid foundation is to focus on what you expect the person to achieve, especially important if you are talking about someone you will work closely with, or who will be responsible directly to you. What value will they add to the 'team' and what do you expect in the way of performance? It is less important in certain areas, but generally, to focus on customer care in vital, and is becoming more the case.

Advertising

The whole point of advertising is to get lots of people interested in the job. There are benefits of promotion from within, but in the majority of small companies, this is not an easy option. If you need to think too hard about it, the chances are you haven't got the right person. Back to basics.

Advertising for jobs is a skill that many ignore. I believe that you must think of two people in this, you and the reader. Too often the job spec is badly written or too technical or it just sounds boring. That, or you write the advert to attract a group of people but do not allow for their needs. A classic is the ad for part-time female staff roles, many of which start at 8 o'clock. What about their kids? Do you need them at 8 or is that just habit? The chances are that you can make it difficult to get the right staff, just by badly thought through details.

Also consider whether you are asking too much from one person, and go a detail too far, stopping good people from applying! Are you likely to find many people with just that combination of skill? Would it not be better to ask for the correct attitude to work, and resign yourself to having to train in some areas? It may be cheaper and more effective in the longer term if you employ the right person, rather than chase a transitory idea of skills needed at the moment.

Where you advertise will depend upon the type of person you need. Be aware of how you judge local papers and media, and act accordingly. The local employment office (known in the past as the labour exchange) has changed, and is a much more professional source of candidates, as many people with excellent qualities find their jobs vanishing beneath them. Also think about using agencies for a number of reasons – it may be cheaper in the long term to use temporary staff (but do not be sucked into allowing them to almost evolve into regular staff). Remember that the expertise of agencies, while adding to employment costs, may reduce the risk of expensive mistakes (but remember to stay in control).

Picking the right one.

Making the right decision is crucial, and you have only got the one choice! But remember that you are also on show, and they are making a choice of you! The right person is the right match, both ways.

Interviews are always an opportunity for a candidate to excel, but more often the small business person shows his or her own weaknesses by doing all the talking. "She really understood the business," was the response at one interview I sat in on (as an observer). Unfortunately, few questions had been asked (and these had been fielded well), and the interviewer spent most of the time talking.

In the end, there are just a few key issues. Can the candidate do the job, and how do they measure up to others? To find this out, estimate the likeliness of success in the role and stick to some well thought out questions so that everyone gets the same chance.

Interviewing

Such an important skill receives little training or preparation. Many people simply assume that they can ask searching questions. Here are some tips.

- Think of a structured set of questions that reflect precisely what you want to find out.

- Prepare the room, and avoid interruptions. Do not create a bad impression of yourself.

- Build a sense of understanding, let your interviewees relax and show themselves at their best.

- Encourage them to talk, avoid doing so yourself as much as possible; be natural and speak naturally.

- Ask leading, open questions that encourage longer, descriptive answers. Avoid questions that merely excite a yes or no answer.

- Maintain control over how the time is spent – don't do as many do, and let the conversation wander, then run out of time.

- Before you see anybody, think how you are going to judge candidates objectively. Be fair to them and in the end you will be fair to yourself. References are a subject apart, but I would not give a reference unless it was good, so I question their value.

- If you want to use fancy tricks such as personality tests, get help.

Making the offer

Yep, that's him – a carefully considered decision! "Can you start Monday?" Not the best way to proceed if you want to look professional, but then you don't always have to stick by the rules. If you really hit it off with someone, then do what you feel is right, but cover your tracks well and do not put yourself to be in a potentially compromising position.

Anybody worth their salt will want a formal offer at some stage, and it is legally required that you write to the successful candidate setting out particulars of the terms of employment, whether or not they are part-time, if they are going to be employed for over 1 month. And you must do this within 8 weeks of their starting. Not to do so can drop you in deep mire later on. If you need help, or think you may, then get help – it saves trouble later.

Early days

The first few hours, days and weeks of a person's employment set the tone for what is to follow. So, as my grandmother used to say, "Start as you mean to go on." Establish your relationship quickly, know what you want, and go about setting in motion the way that you want the new starter to behave.

If a new employee, at whatever level, only knows one way of doing something – the way set out at interview or perhaps before starting – then they will not think to do it differently. There is no point in telling the newcomer to arrive at 10am on the first day if the normal start is 8.30am, even if it is inconvenient to you on that occasion. It sends all the wrong messages about you, your expectations and your own time discipline.

How do you keep going?

Employees do not have the same priorities as you, even though they may be great to work with. They have lives outside of work. It sometimes seems unfair, because you feel at times you have to put them first. But in the end, you must acknowledge that they live for themselves and deal with you (most often fairly) as it suits. If you keep this in mind, it stops you making the classic mistake – getting too close to your staff. How often I see this, even where people work very closely as the business starts but then begin to grow apart later.

If you remember this, you will maintain a more professional relationship based around what you expect. Mixing social life with business life again spells trouble – it makes it harder to criticise their work and worse, 'can' or discipline them when you need to. Communication, motivation and contribution are all interlinked, and must stay in the mind as you move forwards. If staff feel you are being secretive, they are less likely to be open with you, especially as the younger business moves forward. Staff feel motivated by being valued.

Always have high standards for yourself and others, and never let standards slip. When they slip once, they are just about impossible to reinstate without problems and aggravation, which you don't need. Give targets, expect jobs done by certain times, keep an eye on things so that you show interest in their work, and make sure they work for you – not for themselves.

One example of how abuse can start is in a local shop where, because the staff are not managed, there is little control. I know that at least two part-time staff members spend much of their time working for themselves, telephoning clients, doing projects and even helping themselves to materials. But when I mentioned this indirectly to the owner, all he could say was that they are nice girls. And of course they are, but they are human too.

There are other aspects to employment you must be aware of, and these are even trickier. You must always act properly because, if ever you fall out with a staff member, they have very long memories, and if you don't do things right, they have the book of rules on their side. Recently I spoke to Paul, owner of a really good company who has a reputation for being 'over' fair. He treats all employees well, and with Rob was especially generous. He bought him out of his share of the business and wrote off a big debt he had run up, gave him a lump sum and parted company friends. Then the employment services took over, perhaps aided by Rob's wife, asking for the paperwork explaining why he was out of work. Paul fought a claim for unfair dismissal. Paul didn't do things the right way. So be careful, follow the rules (especially the legal ones) to the letter, and don't be too generous as you can set yourself up for a fall.

Parting friends

Never think that when you part company with staff they will stay friends. In 9 cases out of 10 they will not. There are times, especially when you didn't start the right way, that you must part company with staff, however nice they may be. Often it's the least painful option in the longer term, rather than working with what seems to develop into an open sore.

Put another way, you may find that performance doesn't match up to your expectation, and you are becoming increasingly frustrated that your efforts to help staff members improve go unheeded. Or plain dishonesty or other bad conduct means the end of the association, or the job just becomes redundant, or for some other valid reason you feel it is necessary to get rid of the person. There will come a time when you reach a point of despair with some staff.

Do not feel, as many employers do, that their future is your responsibility. Do not feel that you have no options. Do not leave it too long before making painful decisions. Please be careful how you go about it, and as always, take advice about your particular circumstances.

A local company had on their staff a female machinist, employed from when the company started, to do one particular job. Employing her was a mistake that this company did nothing about. They just kept her on and watched as her performance went from bad to worse. Yes, she did a good job, but only when she did it, which was not very often. The trouble was that they did not address the problem, and her attitude started affecting every staff member. Problems compounded. The lady owner asked me for help, and I felt she had a strong case so I put her in contact with an adviser. The problem was not only a common one; it was one where there was a simple solution. Janet just had to state her expectations of performance and set in motion the disciplinary procedure. The focus for the staff member became 'work or go' in nice words. Staff are expected to work for their pay, although not like slaves.

This is the point – there is no such thing as an insurmountable staff problem, but you must go about solving it in the right way. There are various forms of advice from the Citizens Advice Bureau and ACAS, through commercial advisers, various trade bodies who offer this service and solicitors. Loads of people to talk to, and if you're unsure, then a good starting point will be the Enterprise Agency. Business Link is also a source of help.

The same is true for those times when you have staff, good or bad, but work dries up and you have not got enough for them to do. Never feel that you should hang onto staff because you like them, or that it'll get better in the future. Too many companies have felt obliged to put off the dreaded day, to their cost. If you are over-staffed, this is a problem that has knock-on effects. It saps your cash, it destroys morale (as everyone waits for the inevitable) and performance goes down. You take on the air of a failing company and slowly customers start to move away. It is bad news.

The way I have taken to looking at my relationship with staff is, no matter how much I like them, what would be their reaction when they decide they've had enough and want a change. Will they stay with me just to help, because it's me? I doubt it. I am loyal to staff, but ultimately my loyalty must be to me, my business, my family and anything else I hold dear. Staff comes some way down the list.

How to deal with it? Like all things to do with employment, this is a legislative minefield, and you must be careful – you should take advice. That advice is not expensive, but taking it could save you a fortune!

This chapter has made employment sound a difficult area. In fairness it is not, but the more thought given to how you go about this, the better. Good planning saves major problems, but these problems do not happen all the time, indeed seldom do. It's just that when they do they are memorable, but for the wrong reasons. If you do it properly, then employment of the right staff can well be the key that unlocks your future growth potential!

12

Ways to Increase Your Profits

All businesses can improve. The objective of every business must be to make a profit, but for many the profits being made at the moment are not enough. For businesses doing well – more importantly for your business if it is struggling – here are some easy tips for increasing the profit you make, and things to keep an eye on before problems arise.

None of these tips should be used without you thinking how to adapt them. The "They won't work for me!" rubbish that I hear really cuts no ice. These ideas will work, given thought. That's the hard part, getting you thinking how to make it happen for yourself. The tips that follow are but the tip of the iceberg!

All this is only about the application of common sense. There is nothing especially clever about it.

Pareto, the 80/20 rule

In life there are a few basic rules which always seem to hold true. It can form the basis for some simple yet very effective analysis of what you must start to do to improve.

- 80% of sales (volume or value) will come from 20% of customers.

- 80% of hassle will come from 20% of customers.

- 80% of the waste will come from about 20% of the stations or people.

- 80% of your poor payers are in 20% of your customers.

- 80% of your time is spent on 20% of the market.

- 80% of your turnover comes from 20% of your products.

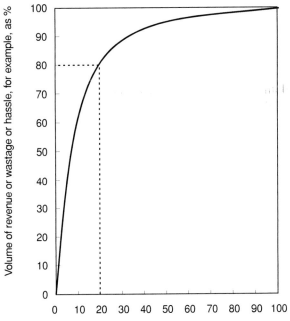

Pareto's 80/20 Law

The most benefit can be gained from a little effort. The hardest part is just starting, getting going and gaining a little momentum. The benefits will come more quickly than you imagined. You will get 80% of the benefit from 20% of the effort.

From my own experience, whenever we made an effort to get things working better, it always surprised me how keen others were to make suggestions – staff and customers alike. The benefits were many

– staff often came up with easier, cheaper solutions, customer loyalty was maintained because they felt a part of what we did, and we found that customers spent more as they felt we listened to them and did not abuse them.

Offer what customers want

It is said that the customer is king, but how often do you ask the customer what he or she really wants? It may be packaging, it will very likely be service. It is always quality.

It is not enough simply to satisfy your customers – which is just giving them what they paid for. You must be **delighting** your customers. That way, they come back to you every time, and will advertise you free to over a dozen friends or colleagues.

Recently I heard of a fish and chip shop that closed. Their main market was the lunchtime trade, and until a short while ago, they prospered. A competitor opened offering lunchtime specials – smaller portions at a reduced price. The people running the 'established' business that failed still say that the customers went because of price. Not necessarily so – nowadays, people don't eat as much at lunchtime and most people hate to waste food. The established 'chippy' lost out because he couldn't see that the shift was definitely towards smaller portions, almost irrespective of price. He could have denied the competition the opportunity.

Do not try to force your customer to have what you want them to have. Gone is the legendary era of Henry Ford when you could have any colour as long as it was black. Do not just follow the herd. Look for new avenues to explore and exploit. Add value in what you do to enhance the service and appeal to customers. Try new sizes or colours. Design changes (fashion makes last year's clothes almost unwearable even though they are perfectly good and serviceable), technology moves on, new ideas come. Every product and service has a life-cycle, so try to spot trends before they happen and stay in front.

Exploit the full potential from customers

It is always easier to sell to existing customers than to get new ones. The hardest sale is the first one. But all customers have a range of needs, so look at it from their point of view – if one good supplier can deal with a range of services, so much the better. Furthermore, the trend is to cut down the number of suppliers and work closer to those who are trusted. If you don't look at ways to expand your service to existing customers, then other businesses will grow at your expense.

Taking the customers' perspective will also allow you to develop your business in other ways. Your business will grow almost automatically. What one customer wants will generally be needed elsewhere too. The best source of ideas is ... the customer.

In my business, we grew in this way. One day another caterer let a customer down for an event and we were asked to step in at short notice. We worked with the client to improve the service. Instead of the buffet food taking customers away from the sales staff, we took the food to them, using waitresses. The client was delighted, the guests were happy, the event cost less, and we made more profit. The first event became many more with that client, and others. Everyone benefited except the first caterer who couldn't see what the customer wanted.

Use your network of contacts

Networking is a key to unlocking hidden sales potential, and whole businesses have been built up around the power of networking, Amway being a good example. You will be positively surprised by the number of people you know – friends, family, contacts, colleagues – it is astonishing how big your network could be.

    Try this little exercise. List out family members, uncles, aunts, cousins, nephews, nieces, in-laws (and their family) and close family friends. Then any other close links from these family members – if you don't know them, just ask.

    Now list your friends going as far back as you can – you and your partner. Start with good friends then gradually move to those you know less well.

    Then list those you have met through work or in business.

Next, list local people in clubs, schools and shops. You will probably have hundreds of contacts. You already know these people, so selling to or through them should not be too hard. Spread the word.

Use contacts quite openly, they will most often be only too pleased to help. Do not be embarrassed – if you think that you provide good service, do a good job and add value, why shouldn't they benefit from your help. It is always easier for people to trust and support people they already know.

Referrals – ask for business

There can be no better accolade than the praise of somebody who is prepared to recommend you. So, when you have finished a job and have built up a good relationship with one customer, or even if you have just been paid, ask if there is anyone else whom the customer thinks would value your service. Many customers are only too happy to help, or too embarrassed not to. It is easy once you get used to doing it! Why stop at one referral – ask for 3 or 4 and also ask if you can use your customer's name. Be open. Few will refuse even if not totally happy and sheer laziness will stop them blocking the opportunity.

The value of referred business is obvious. You are already over the first hurdle of proving you can satisfy customers. Moreover, the person who recommends you has probably given you a lead that he or she at least considers hot!

In the world of finance, the whole industry is geared to referrals. After each sale from an insurance salesperson, you will be asked for two referrals! And why not?

Prune out bad customers

Not all customers are good, as you will recognise. Based on Pareto, about 80% of your profits will come from 20% of your customers, so many of your customers are not making you any money – quite the reverse. Go back through your records (if you have any or if you can). Perhaps it's 70/30 or 90/10, but in general the rule holds true!

Most customers will be around average, but there will always be a rump, which, no matter what you do, will always be bad. They will always want variations, small order values and size, they will demand long credit terms, expect a Rolls Royce for the price of a mini and always complain of the service almost on a point of principle.

Prune them out, albeit carefully. Only keep them if you have a very good reason. It is a hard decision, as it needs courage to turn your back on customers who try to make it sound as if you depend on them. But once made, it is a surprisingly easy decision to maintain and profits will soon improve. As well as this, time and resources can be devoted to expanding your business rather than dealing with problems. As an afterthought, you may well find that, rather than you being dependent, it is they that are dependent on you, and you can then choose whether to deal with them on YOUR terms.

A good example of this in operation came from Paul, a friend of mine, whose company wiped out their overdraft, reduced stock levels and retail prices, making the parts more attractive, and their profits increased dramatically. Actually, sales didn't decrease at all in reality. Paul stands by his decision and his business is now twice as big and ten times more profitable.

It may not seem the right route for you, but the logic is clear. There will be a way for you to prune, or at least decide positively why you want to keep difficult customers – maybe they don't know the bad effect they're having. Let the bad customers go to your competitors and cause them problems instead!

Quality, get it right

Not getting things right first time is a major problem. There are many costs hidden in poor quality. Everything you do in business has a cost, even if it is hidden, and if you do things badly there are many hidden and unnecessary costs.

Rework and scrap are obvious, but what about lost future orders, time wasted dealing with upset customers, unnecessary letters and phone calls, wasted time in re-visits, accidents caused by carelessly discarded rubbish. Waste, rejects and inspection (why inspect if you are confident it's right) are classic examples. Cut out wasted effort.

Do things right first time.

A basic rule in business is that everything costs money – there is no such thing as a free lunch. The very idea that this is not true is laughable. Indeed, many people in large bureaucratic organisations make a lifetime career out of finding things to do to fill up their time. As Parkinson's Law famously states – work increases to fill the time available.

The ideal of course, is to do things right first time. That is the secret of controlling costs.

The Green agenda

In the recent past, it was often assumed that to think green was a nonsense, that green issues were a fad that would one day go away. No longer.

Today, we have put environment high on the agenda, and as resources become increasingly scarce, the issue will gain importance. Every aspect of everything costs. All the things you throw away have an impact on your bottom line. It costs to buy, and it costs to throw away.

A smaller organisation can plan to use wisely, but as your company grows, especially if you are in certain trades, then this becomes difficult, but still necessary. Looked at creatively, there are many ways where even the most unusual (or unwanted) products can be seen to have a use or value.

Simple examples are everywhere. How many offices have all the lights on irrespective of the need, or heating full on with all the windows open? Why are several offices used when one will do? Why is there so much unnecessary duplication of resources, buying in bulk (to get discounts) when the stuff will sit on shelves for ages?

I do not know the answers, but we should all ask the questions. I am like you, but I see the problem coming. It can only get worse, with costs going up, taxes on waste (perhaps indirect) and increased bad publicity. Perhaps here lies an almost immediate benefit. If you are aware of these problems and are doing your best, why not shout about it – with the definite chance that good publicity will bring improved turnover.

Buy a Trumpet, and learn to use it

In business as in life generally, success brings success. People want to deal with successful people and successful businesses. It makes them feel confident in you, and if you are successful, you will exude confidence. But how is anyone going to know if you are successful unless you say so?

If you have a success story, something that makes you special, shout about it. If not, look for one – I bet that you could find plenty to shout about if you want to.

Perhaps one of the best known examples is Richard Branson and the Virgin brand name. We all know Richard's business interests, and all wish him success – well most of us do. The brand is interwoven with the individual who gets a great deal of media coverage, so therefore does Virgin, and all for free.

Advertising, make it work for you

The people who seem to make most money out of advertising are advertising agents – and the media you advertise with. It seems to me that, despite the assurances of advertising sales staff, advertising does not really work as well as promised unless you have an enormous budget.

The purpose of advertising is either to ask for an order or to make people aware of a name. In the first case, how much does each order generated cost you (in terms of the price of the ad) and could there be cheaper, more effective ways to progress? In the second, can you remember from one day to the next many of the advertisements you saw. Brand awareness can cost a lot of money and perhaps there are more effective ways for advertising your goods or services, for example radio (expensive), large posters which are passed daily or PR campaigns in the local press (which are much cheaper if more selective).

Try to find out which of your published advertisements are effective. Code them with phrases such as "Ask for Jane" or "Quote number xx" to tell you which advert an order comes from. Be sceptical when the advertising space salesgirl says with all seriousness, "We have 20,000 readers." It could mean they distribute 20,000 copies, have no readers and only survive on the advertising space sold. You must be cynical as well as optimistic.

Richard Branson now spends about half as much on advertising as he did some while ago and sales have not dropped. In fact they've improved. The benefit of PR for Richard is that he is getting across a message and a story, far more memorable than a few words in a printed box. Richard is communicating rather than just asking for orders.

Discounting – don't give away profits

Everybody wants you to lower your price, but have you thought what happens if you do? What impact do discounts have on your business?

With discounts, costs stay the same, income comes down, so your profits must be reduced by exactly the same amount as you give in discount. You give away your profit. And do you end up selling more? Chances are that you do not. Once you give a discount, then you will always give discount. It is a slippery slope.

If your price is high enough to allow you to discount, either you do not need to read this section or your price could be so high it is losing you work – and perhaps you should be having a more thorough look at your costs!

A point worthy of note and certainly worth your thought is the effect of your reducing your price 'to buy turnover'. Think what your competitors will do. The chances are they will respond the same way, and may even force you to give yet more away! What effect will this have? Simply that everyone loses. The only way you can cut price and stay profitable is to cut costs (often quality suffers) or get really efficient (and you should be that anyway).

Price is about balance, and if you have your figures right, then discounting can be a fool's paradise. But salespeople use it as a way to make their job easier.

A variation of this is the salesman's wheeze of asking the customer how much room they have got to negotiate. They never do negotiate – they give maximum discount to make it easier to get orders. They are, in effect, being paid to give away your profits ... or worse. Take discretionary discounts away, train your sales team (if you have one) to sell, not take orders, and concentrate on value, not cost.

Stay in control of costs

From the outset, you have to be careful of costs. Every penny counts. When you start out, you will probably have tight budgets. Being careful is easier. New businesses are generally very aware of where every penny goes – this does not mean that money is spent wisely, only that spending is easier to see.

As time progresses, this stops. It amazes me how few people in business seem to see that the more they spend, the less profit they have. If they can see, they don't act that way. In business, everything should be reduced to the lowest common denominator – cash. Dave complains of poor cash flow yet drives a Porsche.

Remember that what you get in, less what you spend, is profit. The easiest thing for you to question is why money is being spent. So why do so many people get out of the habit? Here are some of the common causes of unnecessary high cost:

- You build in comfort factors (more stock, an extra person, spare capacity in case of a rush order that never happens).
- You stop looking at things in terms of what they cost.
- You don't want to sack an inefficient worker because he or she's nice, has problems at home, etc.
- You don't look at costs until the money is spent, so the things you make or buy are over-specified and too expensive – costs are hidden.
- You are too busy looking at sales to worry about costs.
- You don't see the cost of quality and don't get it right first time.
- The sales price makes no allowance for all the costs.
- You are confident that you staff will never abuse your trust.

It all boils down to simple logic at the end of the day. The less you spend for any given level of sales, the greater your profit will be. The problem is not the spending, because if you don't spend you don't do anything. It's what you spend, why, what you anticipate getting back and when. Stay in control.

Productivity

Productivity is no more than value for money from your time or your staff. Many forget that you pay for others, and that if you want to get value for the time you spend then you must be in control of it. Time must be managed.

Indeed, time is the one resource that can never be replaced, so make the most of it.

There is nothing that cannot be improved, especially the amount that you can get from time and resources, by planning what you are going to do in the time available. The secret for improvement is really quite simple. The majority go through life doing a reasonably good job, but without focus, they will only achieve a percentage of what they could achieve. This is not work-study, it is simply common sense and human nature. Most people do what they feel is a good job, and they work hard, as they see it.

It is not until you start to measure what you are getting from your own and staff's time that things start to improve – most often because it becomes a focus. You start to highlight wasted time, unproductive work, unnecessary jobs, and wasted effort. So simple measures will bring with them many subtle and unseen benefits.

A classic case of innocent wasting of time can be seen in the busiest of offices, and it is done without any malice, nor even recognition that it is even happening. This example was chosen, not because I am picking on offices – it happens everywhere. Many roles start as part-roles that fill in for other, overworked staff. As a result, there is often plenty of time during the day that has filler jobs or meetings with other staff around issues that in a busy office would be ignored. These filler jobs then take on their own importance. Reports that are never used, information seldom read except by those for whom it is not intended, regular review meeting from which nothing important ever emerges.... And so on. It is known as make-work.

In the most blatant example, an office of one seriously underworked secretary resulted in her getting bored and very lonely. As a result, she spent ages on the phone running up unnecessary bills talking to friends everywhere. Her employers felt she must be really busy (always on the phone) and so were talking about getting an assistant to help her cope!

Keep staff busy and watch what they produce. Do not listen to them simply talking about how busy they are. That is simply being a 'busy fool'. Watch what they produce.

Check deliveries and invoices

Many supermarket customers check the receipt even though they see the items being scanned through the checkout. It's their money and so they want to be confident that even automated systems do not make a mistake.

But when it comes to work, orders are handled at a distance and the whole process becomes much slacker. "Sign here, I've left the stuff in the foyer." And people sign, often without checking what they're signing for.

It is important to check the details of price and volume, and that all is as ordered. If not, and there is a mistake, you have only yourself to blame if you did not check carefully as the goods were being delivered. Imagine the situation – the order is vital for an important contract and some of the parts are not there. The person that is left carrying the can is most often you. Who pays? It's got to be you.

Outsourcing, why make when you can buy better for less

Outsourcing (as it has become known) is an important thing to remember – as I have learned to my cost. If you can get it better and cheaper by buying it in, so that you concentrate where you are good, then outsourcing can only be a source of benefit to you.

Pride, not understanding and laziness are some of the main reasons why outsourcing is not used, especially in smaller businesses. There are areas where you need to keep control of supply, but even this does not say it requires to be done by you. Price, quality and delivery are all issues you can manage. You have to do what is right in your circumstances, but common sense tells me that you are best concentrating on what you do best.

In my case, our company developed a range of cakes which complimented our main lines. Making these cakes was always a major disruption of what we otherwise did and required that we should employ staff just for them. We decided that we would contract a supplier to make them by providing the recipes and specific equipment needed. The product was as good as we could make, cost less to make and didn't tie up our facilities.

Manage your time

Managing time is a difficult skill to acquire. To rush around 'putting out fires' is easy, and it is hard to see that you are really wasting time and money. After all, you are solving problems, aren't you? But, far better not to have fires to put out, or train your staff to put them out for you before they become raging infernos.

Be careful with your time and delegate the problem to where it originated if at all possible. Set aside time for dealing with routine issues before they become crises; keep meetings short and stick to agendas. When someone brings you a problem, ask for an answer as well.

A simple philosophy I hold dear is that, as a boss, it is important that you delegate as much as possible – even to clients! The benefits are many and varied, even if the hardest part is letting go. You will always think you do something better than a staff member, but think how hard a person will work to turn their idea into reality. Think of how much your clients will like what you make if they are closely involved in the design!

Stocks – dead money just sitting around

Controlling stocks is always easier planned than done. The temptation is always to have too much sitting on the shelf ... just in case. But stock is like dead money just tied up and not earning you anything in return. It's as though you have piles of £10 notes just lying around. Free up as much as you can.

Stocks can build up in many areas:

- *Raw Materials* – Buy only what you need. Most suppliers will be flexible on deliveries. It may cost a small amount more, but the savings to you can be significant. What if one part becomes obsolete and you have large stocks?

- **Work in Progress** – This is hidden stock and the costs can be quite horrendous. It causes confusion, things get lost, quality can deteriorate and it can even be downright dangerous. It can seriously damage the health of any organisation!

- **Finished goods** – This is a complex area and some customers may expect you to hold certain stock levels for them or have deliveries on sale or return – as good as stock. Whatever the cause, do not have more stocks than you need. Make to the shortest lead-time possible.

Collect the money – it's yours after all

There are many in business who complain about poor payers and bad debts. They are the curse of businesses everywhere and some of the largest companies are the poorest payers!

In reality, people owing you money is like your being a free bank. You are financing somebody else's business or their lifestyle! History is littered with poor payers. It is also littered with the results of poor payment, and the many companies who have gone out of business as a result. The stresses at a business level are bad enough – at a personal level they are dreadful.

Here are a few tips that may help:

- Add in an amount for interest for late payment – this is the price, good for so long and then the price goes up. Perhaps simpler, if you know a customer is going to be late, simply charge more in the first place! Do you want to sell things at a loss?

- Many larger companies and authorities pay on the third invoice (thinking that invoices come every month). Send a reminder every week! If you don't ask you won't get, and there's nothing to stop you bucking the system.

- Explore factoring, even debt collection if things get really bad. It may cost you some, but at least you get your money and can use the money to grow (or go on a well-deserved holiday).

- Personal contact, sitting in the debtor's office, works well. It brings on guilt for them, and often they pay up.

- You must be seen to ask for your money, and be firm that you will be paid. As a last resort, there are the courts, not an easy option, but there even for small companies. Big companies and authorities use them at will, so why shouldn't you. Get creative with how you use the courts. Once I had a poor payer, so rather than go the normal way to get repayment, I got a garnishee order on his biggest client to pay me. Not only did I get my money, he also lost his customer, so it cost him dear in the end.

Keep things Simple and Straightforward

Known as the KISS approach (once used by IBM as a warning to their telephone users to 'keep it simple, stupid!'). Because of the complexity of your problems, nobody ever understands them and therefore never really solves them. Poppycock! Get the basics right. Keep It Simple and Straightforward so that everybody can understand. The person most likely to exaggerate your problems is you.

KISS is a very powerful ideal to help keep your eyes on what is important. Watch the things that matter. Remember Pareto?

As a business adviser, I am often confronted with clients saying that I don't understand their business so cannot possibly understand nor see the way out of the mess they have created for themselves. Maybe that is the case in nuclear physics or some advanced medicines. Staying away from the detail makes it only too easy to see where they have gone wrong.

People can only deal with a few facts at a time – too many details clutter the issue. For most people, eight bits of information is the most they can handle. Too much detail and decisions become harder, not easier. The natural reaction is that you look for more information, but you will not be able to decide and will then want even more information. Too much and you will run away from decisions, as they become harder, not easier. You will become an ostrich, and you will bury your head in sand.

The trouble with detail is that it assumes an importance far greater than it deserves. So when you use detail, use it as wisely as you can. Don't just have facts floating around.

So to finish, action not words.

Having been given some pointers as to where you can look for ways to improve without too much effort, the thing to do now is actually start doing something. Remember Pareto – 80% of the benefit will come from just doing something about the problems! Make a start, but go about things in a structured way if possible.

Good intentions come to nothing. Be definite on what you are going to do, write it down and review progress with somebody. This plan of action will be much more valuable than you think, as it will also form a record of progress and achievement. Success brings success, and success in even one area will encourage you.

13

The One-Percent Rule

There is not likely to be one single answer to improving performance and profitability. Poor performing companies, and those that are failing, look for the magical golden answer to all their prayers. Be it a new salesman, a new computer, a better office, a new product or a new control system. Absolute rubbish – it's none of these, it's about the basics of business and doing it better. There is no one answer, but there is a way forward.

To start, let's return to the basic understanding of what profit actually is. In simple terms (and let's not confuse things), it's income less costs. It stands to reason then that to improve profits requires that you increase income and decrease costs. 'That's obvious!' I hear you say, but how do you do it?

Well, if you just try to improve sales, the chances are you won't succeed. And if it's just cost cutting, then you will probably do as most do, slash costs and end up going out of business because you are unable to sustain the business on the reduced turnover that's almost sure to come. There is no one easy answer to your prayers, and the chances are you've got into a mess because you've taken your eye off the basics.

Before I show you a worked example of how effective small changes can be, let me stress that you must be looking for action. Action to improve turnover, action to improve productivity, action to improve efficiency, action to improve quality and action to reduce waste. The by-word is action, and action is key. Remember Pareto and the 80:20 rule, you will get most of the benefit just by doing some simple things. It certainly holds true in this context.

Equally important, if you are in trouble or just want to do better (as should be the case anyway), then you must have a questioning mind. I always thank the course tutor on my MBA when he summed up the value of the course.

"You will know many fancy theories, and have lots of ideas implanted into your mind. But if, when you leave this place, you have learned to ask the simple question 'Why?', then this course will have been a success. Keep asking why until you come to the stage where somebody cannot give a good answer, then you will have come to the truth."

Seldom have I heard more profound words for business.

Let me take the accounts from a friend's business as an example of how the one-percent rule might work. Admittedly, my friend has been in business a while, so the numbers are a little bigger than many new start-ups, but the principle is the same. The numbers are, for convenience, set out like an accountant would set out your accounts after your first year. Same idea. Turnover less purchases gives gross profit, gross profit less expenses gives what's left – and that's profit (if there is a profit).

**Profit and Loss Account
for the year ended 31 March 1999**

		£
Turnover		289 745
Cost of sales (purchases to us)		123 245
Gross Profit		166 500
Expenses		
Salaries	42000	
Wages	55350	
Advertising	8565	
Stationery	635	
Rent and rates	11575	
Telephone etc.	5350	
Light and heat	2300	
Motor	7500	
Insurance	1375	
Bank	1690	
Audit and accountancy	2310	
Admin (postage etc)	1200	
		139850
Operating Profit (the important bit left)		**26650**

I realise that there are other elements to take into account, like tax, but this is the important information. How could my friend go about improving the business, and what effect could it have? Let's take it bit by bit, item by item. We won't worry about accounting niceties, just look at the overall picture. Actually, Jeff is following this process, and it is working.

Turnover

Jeff has concentrated on the front end of the sales cycle, and is getting to see more customers. Because of this, despite there being a 'squeeze' in the market as competition gets tough, there are several new customers and several more customers understand that Jeff can actually do more for them than they thought. Part of the secret has been that he has not discounted as much as he did before (he still does a bit), and has improved his delivery reliability, thus being seen to give better service (which was very important to one major customer). Sales have risen by over 1.5% to £295,105.

Purchases

Reducing purchases was a problem to start, and because Jeff uses specialist suppliers, it seemed difficult to crack. Two issues have helped. The use of the Internet on his computer at home found alternative suppliers, and he has slightly reduced his use by reducing scrap. This last issue was not thought to be a problem until he looked at breakages. He has reduced the costs of the goods he sells by a little under 1%. The cost now is £122,355, still an improvement.

Salaries

This is what Jeff takes out of the pot, and here there has been no reduction. The nice thing is that Jeff is now earning his keep, and looking for ways to improve, so what he takes out is better justified.

Wages

Nobody likes taking a cut in wages, and people here were the same as everywhere else. Working less weekend time and less overtime made cuts. Better productivity meant that more work was done in the normal day, and there was better efficiency by thinking ahead of time to see problems and issues coming. Savings, rather than rises, although not major, were made easier because no one person bore the brunt of the pain, everybody hurt just a bit – but now enjoy more time off! Jeff saved £1,225, and this year wages are down to £54,125.

Advertising

This is an area where bigger cuts were made, but nobody has noticed any lower sales as a result. Although it will take some time for all the savings to come through, Jeff has saved £2,500 with one advertiser, and to compensate, has been more aggressive in his use of PR. To enable him to find the adverts that worked, Jeff built codes into the adverts he ran such as 'Ask for Julie' and similar. This last year, Jeff has only spent £6,065 on advertising, and says, "It's better in my pocket than theirs!"

Stationery

It's just about impossible to find if Jeff has used more or less stationery, because it's not one of those things that is bought for the year. Actually, Jeff's bill for stationery has increased, not by much, but now stands at £680. It will not break the bank, but there is opportunity through less use of paper items. Jeff could rely far more on his computer and try to move to a paperless environment, but not yet!

Rent and Rates

Again, no reduction, but for some reason, no increase either.

Telephone

Jeff has made what he sees as quite a saving here and again this is down to discipline, actually thinking ahead and not making unnecessary calls. Early on in the year, Jeff realised that when he was idle, his first instinct was to pick up the phone. He used his own daily 'To do list' which helped him take control of his time and, when he had spare moments, he would tackle these jobs rather than sit on the phone. He had originally excused this by saying he was chasing orders, but in reality he was not. The phone bill came down to £4,370.

Light and heat, Motor, Insurance

These, together with all the rest came to similar amounts in total, although the individual areas did vary, although not by much. The biggest savings were in bank costs through better management of his finances, and saving the odd occasion where he went over his limit.

So now the figures look a bit different, even though the accountant has not officially agreed them. But then, like many accountants, Jeff's is a bit slow, a service industry which could certainly improve the service it offers.

**Profit and Loss account
for the year ended 31 March 2000**

		£
Turnover		295105
Cost of sales (purchases to us)		122355
Gross Profit		172750
Expenses		
Salaries	42000	
Wages	54125	
Advertising	6065	
Stationery	680	
Rent and rates	11575	
Telephone etc	4370	
Others	16280	
		135095
Operating Profit (the important bit left)		37655

So we can see that, with a little effort yet no major investment or changes, Jeff has given his business just over £11,000 more profit. Nothing significant was done, there were no major changes, but big improvements. Looking for lots of small improvements, is known as the 'One-percent rule'. Lots of 'one-percents' makes for a big result. Now Jeff was making a good return, his profit was good for the turnover he had achieved in 1999. But he wanted to do better.

There are many businesses that will not make nearly as much as Jeff, and for them, the results can be even more dramatic. The nice thing is that it doesn't take an expert to show you where you could improve, it just takes a bit of courage to look at the way you do things, and admit (and here's the hard part) that you may have been doing it wrong! When I visit companies now, the hardest part is getting them to admit that there may be scope for improvement. It is surprising how many refuse to believe that they're not perfect.

So when it comes to the crunch, where do you stand? Will you stand for vanity, and believe you are perfect and that it's just bad luck that your business is not doing as well as Bloggs and Co. down the road? Or will you at least acknowledge that it is worth looking anew?

Can you afford not to?

14

Who Put the 'E' in Commerce?

www.oldkingcole.co.uk
linden@oldkingcole.co.uk

Recently we have heard much about this thing called the Internet. Only 20 years ago, we were presented with the first word processor. But now I am willing to bet that few people have seen an ordinary typewriter in the recent past. I can remember when Terry, my father-in-law, a dyed-in-the-wool traditionalist, said that these things called computers would "never take off". Some months ago he said that he (well actually Anne, his wife) was on the Internet – without even the slightest trace of embarrassment or confusion. To me, this shows that the Internet has become a fact of life!

The Internet, for all the fuss, is just a means of communication, like the telephone but much more important. The changes it brings though are very fundamental. We can be much more creative in the way we communicate, and that impact has yet to be fully felt. Advertising and marketing will change as we start to unlock the power and economy of what is in effect a free medium. Television and other advertisements now all have 'web addresses', Tony Blair predicts that 10 million jobs will be created through the digital economy and the fastest growing group to use the Internet are 'Silver Surfers'. In the near future, this technology will be an everyday part of life.

It is predicted that some industry groups will be dominated by this new technology, and will account for 65% of e-business. They are cars, retail selling, shipping and transport, industrial equipment, hi-tech and government. But all industries will be turned upside down by technology – much as the telephone overturned communication in the last century. As I write this, the Consumers' Association has started selling cars on the Internet at an enormous discount. I wonder how long traditionalists can come out with all the same old arguments about personal service, especially when, in my experience, service via the Internet is excellent.

The Internet is accurate and cheap. The highest cost is of a local phone-call for as long as you need it. It is easy, reliable, and very open and, yes, it can be secure if you want. On this last point, I have heard it said that the Internet is full of fraud. But how many times have we given our credit card details to a stranger over the telephone, or just signed the slip at the end of a good meal – without even worrying about it?

The growth of Internet use is not in the arena of commerce, it is in those areas that seldom get seen by the public. The Internet touches every part of your business, and it is not until you start to think about it that you begin to understand how fundamental this could be to you.

What is likely to happen in the big wide world?

The pressure is on. If you are somewhere in the supply chain, or if you are about to become a part of it, if you do not really add significant value to your customers, then start thinking about what other business you want to be in. Already I have seen one company whose markets "... just seem to be disappearing – we can't understand it."

In the past, businesses have grown around locations, something that really may have no bearing in the future. Why should I walk from estate agent to estate agent to buy a house, when I can browse details through the Internet. Estate agency as we know it could simply evaporate. Physical location can become a liability, and to a business, it is an overhead cost. The secret will be to give something, to add some value that makes people want to visit you, whether at your website or shop window ... or both. Give a little to get a lot back, rather than (as has happened in the past) trying to be greedy. Whether you need premises for this is up to you to decide.

There are not just threats out there. Some significant opportunities do and will exist, and Internet companies are springing up all around us. New services are becoming possible and the word is 'be quick'. With this revolution, comes the re-emergence of traditional businesses. 'White van man' has made a comeback as delivery and other associated services are becoming more important. Designing websites has become a boom business in itself, and computers are moving quickly – even if they are now becoming so low cost that the profit margins are disappearing.

Recent pressure on the cost of access to the Internet has caused an explosion of interest. The prospect of free access has given a flurry of excitement, and of course, in true tradition, all this free PR has had the effect desired – interest has become intense. The Internet boom has begun to feed itself. It will not go away and so you must be aware of it. It can bring some serious advantages.

There are some areas where the Internet will only be of limited value, but will still have an impact. Selling accounts for only about 10% of where this technology can be used in business. It is used for a wide range of things, such as:

- Purchasing – as you sell, so there are those wanting to sell to you, and you may be able to buy cheaper and better through this medium. You can find buying clubs where small traders group together to get bulk discounts. You may get access to your supplier's supplier, and just deal direct.

- You may start building a good relationship with the most unusual of companies, and that could take your business into all kinds of fields. Keep an open mind.

- The Internet is a wealth of free information. Huge amounts of free data exist in cyberspace, and the question must be, "Why not use it to develop your product?" It is a boost to research and development, and production. No longer do we have the excuse of not knowing how to do something. You can guarantee that you will get information, or at least clues, somewhere.

■ The ease of access and the changes to ways of doing business mean that, through the Internet, you can now drastically reduce your stock levels as lead-time is reduced. It sounds crazy, but I know quite a number of businesses who have done away with stock altogether, and several businesses that have started recently who do not even see the products they are selling.

■ Instant 'on line' banking is now offered by all of the big banks (it is a better service for you and it cuts their costs). You can do everything via your computer, even pay bills or complain about the numbers in your balance. This can (and in many cases does) improve cashflow – it makes cash management easier.

■ Outsourcing is a sticky area, but one with huge potential, especially for new businesses. Many companies grow up having to do everything, simply because they cannot find the right sort of help or because they know no better. It stops many even starting in business in the first place. But you can now access services ranging from administration and accounts to contract management and even stock management. Better, it means that you can start a service business and offer it via the Internet to large numbers who otherwise may not be able to use it. You could even go 'international' without the need for plane fares!

■ Simply communicating via e-mail is quick, easy and guaranteed to get through – provided you know the address. No more "I'm sorry, his number's engaged" or "He's in a meeting." Mind you, as it is easier for you to contact customers and suppliers, so you too can be contacted (and you lose the excuses that typically let you avoid inconvenient contact).

■ As a child, I can remember seeing a space programme where the characters were using a telephone which allowed them to look at the person they were speaking to on a screen. Impossible, this could never happen, I thought. How wrong – videophones are here, and if you are happy to attach them to your computer, dead

155

cheap and easy to use. A colleague has one of these gadgets on his desk – a telephone with a small screen that lets you see who you are speaking to. Outrageous, but think of the potential – you can do international business over the phone, so why bother spending thousands on plane fares?

■ Advertising is just different forms of communication. This new technology can really let you be quite creative and much more effective using this medium than ever you were. A website is an advertisement for your business that is there when people need it, can be easily found and can have an instant response mechanism (even without going as far as e-commerce), all at low cost. Also, it can easily be changed or built upon. What future then, one might ask, for many of the papers and advertising media of the present who rely on advertising revenue to generate their profits – even cover their costs?

■ Marketing also is just letting the market know what you want to tell it. Mailshots, promotions, new brochures can all be set up on the Internet – however you want to put out information, it can be done via cyberspace. The interesting bit comes with the degree of flexibility it lets you have. Suddenly you can have much more professional material put out when you like, and all transmitted for the cost of a local phone-call – and that cost is coming down!

When you start to explore how you can acquire some really effective business benefits, they become obvious. The trouble is that there is so much scope that you will almost be forced into using this medium in some form, just to keep up – and there are some drawbacks that only become apparent when you get going.

The biggest of these is how people actually find you. At the moment, around 90% of websites never get found, because nobody knows who you are, what you do nor how to find you. If your name is Mr Tesco, Mr Virgin, Mr B&Q or even Mr Inland Revenue, everyone knows who you are and how to find you. You are well known and your web address is therefore obvious. If you are able to get a good domain name (more of this later) you stand a good chance. But if you are Bloggs and Co., purveyors of high quality ladies undergarments, at 23 High Street, who is going to know how the devil to find you. There are numerous methods being developed at the moment, but as we go to print, nobody can completely resolve this problem. That is the next hurdle – the technology is there but we are waiting to develop a commercial way to make it work, or alternative approaches to overcoming the problem.

Domain names

This is your identity on the Internet. To the world at large, you can be a famous person, but to the digital world of the Internet, without an identity, you are nobody. This identity is called your domain name. It is vital. Without one, you are not 'on the Net'.

Another disconcerting fact is that you, with a new website, are potentially as big as Microsoft – your identity is only as big as the screen. Consequently, as long as you perform well, your customers need not know that yours is only a one-person business. Indeed, some very big businesses on the Internet employ only a few people.

Who would have thought of major financial institutions calling themselves Goldfish or Egg? I can remember the shock when I first saw these names, and thought they must be raving mad. How wrong I was, and how I wish I could turn back the clock and buy a few of the more unusual names now! These are easily remembered for their very simplicity yet very unusual characteristics. They will not be forgotten, and they are fun. They also mask otherwise boring businesses methinks (sorry, I am not trying to offend bankers, but most non-bankers find banks boring places under normal circumstances).

For my own part, I have bought my own domains. With a name like Cole, it struck me that I should register the name Old King Cole (as in the fairy story about this merry old soul). So now you can reach me by typing linden@oldkingcole.co.uk. I promise that you will always now associate that name with me. How can you develop an identity to allow your customers to always identify what you do with you?

This goes to illustrate the importance of domain names. They are the brand names and brand identities of the future. You need to get a name that is catchy, or a name that is easily remembered, or a name that says what you do. Me, I prefer the catchy ones, but that is choice. Others swear by the ones that describe what you do – and often these can have serious advantages. Take, for example, www.lastminute.com – this is both.

Some talk of the suffixes, such as .com and .co.uk – both of these are okay. They indicate which country you are in. Get advice, but most important, get a name. Go to your local Business Link or Information Society Initiative centre. Names can be bought from as little as £10.55 (at time of print), but can cost you much more. The difference is not the name but where you buy it, so shop around. Advice around anything to do with the Internet abounds, so do not worry, just get moving.

'Tecky Bits' – why worry – just think what you want to do

The majority of people are put off by what they see as a technology thing, part of the mystique put out by those who want to make things sound difficult. Do not worry, and do not let other people bamboozle you. It is not at all difficult.

There is no reason why you need to even get involved with the design and development of the site from a technical standpoint – just worry about what you want to do. Do not take a DIY attitude if you are not confident – you will only do yourself a disservice. However, the technology is now so good that it lets you in large part do what you want – and is being extended daily. A general rule is that those bits that (to us) look hard are in fact easy, and those things that look easy may be a nightmare and can cost an arm and a leg. If what you want will be difficult, find some way to start slowly and build – that way cash becomes less of a problem. You do not need to be perfect.

When designing your website, talk to loads of people who can help, because there are many ways to skin a cat, and they all come at a price. Just tonight (yes, I do burn the midnight oil) I was chatting to a new client who has, on my advice, spoken to about four companies so far. The cheapest price quoted for what will be a biggish website was £2,500. The most expensive was costed at between £15,000 and

£20,000. Her preferred option would cost around £5,000 (give or take a bit) but this supplier really understood what she wanted to do, added loads of great ideas and not only would develop her site, but could do masses of promotion. She felt it was a bargain, and I would agree – I know this designer well.

The lesson is simple – do not be put off. The market is a big one and there are many out there who could help you,

Search Engines – yes more tech. stuff, folks – sorry

I'm not going to spend too much time here, but do need to mention search engines and talk a bit about some important criteria. Search engines are the things that let you find specific information, the more specific the better. If you were to go to your local library and ask the librarians to show you all the information available on a particular subject, they probably would vaguely point at several rows of shelves. Search engines give you a list of all the specific websites that contain the information that you are asking for. All you have to do is click on the chosen name from a long list – and there is your information.

When other people are looking for the information that you have available, your website ideally should come top of the list for them as often as possible.

Search engines are workhorses and make the Internet work for the person looking for information. There are two ways you can be found – either someone types in your name (domain names need to be memorable), or somebody types in what they want, and a search engine goes looking for websites that have got that combination of words.

You must not worry because you don't understand how they work. They are all different. Some search the world for you, others are more like huge directories that you can have your name put into – a bit like yellow pages. Without some method of finding things, it would be impossible to use the Internet, like having telephone numbers but no way of finding out who has got what number!

AltaVista is a massive bank of computers somewhere in California that stores copies of data, and every so often goes looking for more. It is more like a true library of everything that has been put 'on the

Web'. Yahoo is simply a big complicated directory of all the sites that have registered with it. These types are, in reality, more common (Lycos and others included – not trying nor wanting to omit anyone). You also have what are known as Portals (organisations like Telewest, Freeserve and Virgin) who again are directories. They all work differently – you just need to let them know you are actually out there even if you don't understand how they work. Get advice, again from someone like Business Link. They are at least impartial.

What search engines look for

Search engines are the systems that find you if people do not know your name – a bit like yellow pages. For that reason, it really does pay to know how they work, simply so they can work better for you. You don't need the detail, but if you know some of the key ideas in outline, then you will know how to ask for help.

I have said elsewhere that computers are really as 'thick as a plank', and will only do exactly what you tell them to. For example, if you ask them to look for something that contains a spelling mistake, they won't correct the spelling, they will simply look for that. They look for exactly what they've been asked for. Equally, if you don't tell them what is in your site, they see it and won't bother looking.

Metatags are worthy of a mention, simply because they let your website be seen. Many web pages creators either don't seem to know about them, forget to include them, or just make up any old words that seem to come into their heads. Metatags are simply words that the search engines look for when looking for appropriate websites. Metatags can perhaps best be described as little flags that your website waves in order to get noticed. Not using these little flags is like entering a beauty contest but hiding down behind a screen.

Another big mistake that many web designers make is that they ignore the importance of page names. Yes, every web page has got a page name, and these names are important to help being found. Many times I have seen web pages that are titled with replications of the domain names. The names are put on by the person doing the tecky stuff, and they forget that the search engines (that use page names too) don't really care about the person who wrote the information – all they want is the information. The page can tell them what's there, and if you don't tell them, they won't look.

About 60% of people look for information on the Internet by using search engines, and the way they get information is by key words or phrases that point them in the right direction. These come in an order of priority:

1st	**domain names** – if helps if your name includes (in part) what you do. Dot coms get looked for first, then the national sites – for example .co.uk in England, .fr in France and so on – at least that's what the experts have told me, although this seems less important
2nd	**page names** that reflect exactly what you ask for
3rd	**metatags** that match a key phrase
4th	**exact words** or names in the text of the page as a last resort.

The trouble is that the rules change and you need to keep updating your site to reflect this. Search engines used to look for key phrases on the 'home page', but designers got the hang of this and started cheating. Computers don't 'read' the page, they read the digital information that is used to make up the page. So they don't see colours and images like you and I do. Consequently, designers started writing in white on a white background. Of course, you couldn't see it, but the computers could. Then designers went one stage further – they started writing all over the page in many layers. At this, the search engines got fed up and just changed the rules because they were getting serious headaches with people trying to bend the rules to get noticed.

Another way to get noticed is to keep getting noticed. It stands to reason. Computer logic says that if people keep visiting that site, it must be good. So to gain brownie points, they keep going back there, thinking it must be good. Websites that are visited more often get visited more often. The trick then is to get visited often. How can this be encouraged? Get the background work right then encourage people to have a look. You can arrange PR articles, you can advertise your page name, ask friends and customers to 'have a look', and specify this as your own 'home page'. The list of tricks can be long.

A note of caution – if you upset search engines, they can get mighty upset and vindictive. If they think you are trying to manipulate them, then they will put you to the bottom of the pile. Some people do try to get their sites noticed by unfair means, or feel that they know best. This is called 'spamming', and search engines take a dim view of people trying to do this. It can happen without your even thinking about being pushy, such as when you 'post' your site (tell the search engine you're there), and you click the button twice. The search engine will think you are trying to 'spam' it. Really not fair, but easy to do, so be sure to enlist the help of an expert.

Another fatal mistake is to tell the world that your site is 'under construction' – it simply tells the search engines not to come and find you because you're not ready and not worth looking at. It can be hard to recover from this.

Dos and Don'ts

The best way to illustrate this section is to give a good example of a bad website. Please don't go looking for it, because by the time you read this it will have been substantially changed. But, no names now as I don't want to embarrass someone – even though it would be deserved.

The other day, I went to see a client who I had not seen for around 12 months. Someone had offered to build their website for free, for a portion of the income of all the trade they got through their site. If it became busy, then they would pay more, if not then it would not have cost them anything. I was amazed at this negative approach, but I was asked to go and 'have a look' (they thought I would be impressed).

The Internet has made users very intolerant, and this site has all the mistakes. Obviously it had been organised, designed and made by someone who understood the technology, but forgot all about the person using the site. This stood out like a sore thumb. Let me go through the main mistakes in the order I found them.

● The site had a 'front page' saying that the site was under development – bad news as this says that that the visitor is wasting time visiting, and you are telling those all-important search engines not to bother looking for you. The first page actually said nothing, but said it slowly and used lots of words. An invitation to go away.

- The site took ages to load – almost 5 minutes in busy times – for a number of reasons. Most people using the Internet will allow about 15 seconds for a site to load – the Internet makes people impatient. 30 seconds is bad, but 5 minutes! Most people would have left by now.

- When the site loaded, again it was full of words, all really important to the person writing the page but of absolutely no interest to the reader. It just confused and bored visitors. Worse – a revolving movie picture of the shop caused loads of delay but served absolutely no purpose.

- Because of all the clutter, the site was difficult to 'navigate', and made you want to go away.

- I decided that I wanted something, something easy. So, in the place designated, I typed the desired item using the common word for it. Imagine my reaction when I was shown something else. Technically correct? Perhaps, but did I care … not on your life. By now, the site was a challenge to me, but I would never buy.

- So I persevered again and searched on. By now, it was impossible to do business on this site. Eventually though, as much through guile as anything, I found the item, but at a cost of £999.99 – for something which can cost between about £50 and £200.

Ah well, I was disappointed. My client had, in the rush to do the right thing, forgotten one critical factor, the customer who uses the site! My client had forgotten to do it right.

Marketing on the Internet

For some very simple reasons, if you don't tell people that you have a website, it is unlikely people will find it. Yes, we have talked about some of the technical issues, and these help. However, one thing that many people forget is that it is very difficult to use the Internet to market the Internet! That's like building an attractive new store, but building it on Dartmoor. Some people will happen across it by chance, but is that what you want?

The nice thing about marketing your site is that it need not be expensive. It can be, but it need not be. And sometimes the 'cheaper' methods can be more effective. What you must remember about marketing is that you are only communicating to your potential interested public – not the whole world – only your chosen market. Consequently you don't need to pay huge amounts to broadcast what you are doing.

A good example of this is www.headstartonline.com, an educational site set up as a free resource to students and schools to point the way to good educational support websites – places to go to get information and study material. This site, started by two really concerned teachers who wanted to help their students, was frantically looking for funds to advertise their site, and cash is always tight. Yes, they could advertise on the telly, but would that be good value for money? It certainly gave them a headache.

To me though, it could be looked at in a different way. Let technology work for you! They knew that their market was schools and schoolchildren (and consequently parents), and this group has one thing in common. It struck me that this non-profit making site (at present) was a super potential resource and may help. Teachers are crying out for help, and may really welcome this resource. So I suggested they go to their sources, get the e-mail addresses of every school, and send (grouped of course) an e-mail to every school inviting teachers to 'have a look' at the website (obviously with the address given which is an automatic link to the site). Should they think it is of value, then of course all they have to do is let the kids know it's there, and print the attached letter and send it home to parents. Every interested party contacted! Oh yes, the cost. Given a bit of thought and some 'legwork', it would not cost more than a few pence! Simply the cost of one local phone call to send the e-mail.

Marketing on the Internet is not that much different from traditional marketing, except that you can be far more creative, and can use the technology to do much of the work for you. Here are some simple pointers.

☑ Include your website and e-mail address on every single piece of stationery you can, and have it on vehicles and shop windows.

☑ Use PR to talk about your site, and the benefits it may bring. Use trade press and local newspapers, send out cards, use all means possible to make your domain name visible – especially if you have a memorable or intuitive name.

☑ Link your website to those in complimentary groups so that leads come from people elsewhere.

☑ Capture e-mail addresses from customers, suppliers and anybody you meet, so that when needed, you can group them together and be proactive.

☑ Remember that you can send one message to many people at the same time, so you could send a new brochure in electronic form to many potential customers for virtually no cost at all. The same with offers.

☑ The cost of 'above the line' advertising can be substantially reduced, simply because all you need broadcast is the web address, your domain name. "Come visit our website at www....."

☑ Really spend time targeting the customers you want, because the technology now available lets you do just that.

There are several important points about use of the Internet, if you want to get involved, that must underpin everything you do.

▣ Make what you do customer friendly, because if you don't, they won't come back.

▣ Give a little to gain a lot, and don't try to be selfish.

▣ Be ready for the long haul – most of the fortunes from the 'early birds' have already been made.

▣ Try to make people mark your site as one of their favourites – so they keep using your site. Give them something unusual. (An example here is the Vauxhall cars website that had the 'Trafficmaster' map showing the hold-ups on the motorway network. People planning a journey, or wanting to drive back from work can simply go to the site to access traffic information. Every time, they have Vauxhall advertisements and name in front of their eyes.)

▣ Make your website clean, easy, uncluttered and quick.

▣ Tell people where you are – tell everybody – otherwise your website will be just wasted time.

As far as marketing and the Internet are concerned, the whole subject is evolving as we explore the medium of cyberspace. However, you are trying to mark yourself as different, as special. Explore as many links as you can, be creative and offer something special – and to not undersell yourself. Let others do that.

One message is coming through loud and clear – this time the customer really does come first. The message you have got to put out is that you are doing something for them, and that they would want to be a part of it. The customer really is king, and you want them to really feel good.

I could expound for hours, but the evolution of the Internet has brought one thing really to the fore. Have fun, do zany things, be happy and show that you are really enjoying yourself. And let your customers have fun too. Look around various sites and see which ones you enjoy visiting, then learn from that as to what you think your customers will like.

Another case where the message went wrong

I was asked to review a website where a local company was trying to create a 'family album' where you could post your kid's first photos. Their website was an advertisement for this, no more. Who, I wonder, will go 'surfing the web' looking for adverts – I wouldn't. It was a great idea in its potential, but the people approached it from completely the wrong direction. For £30 approximately, you could post your child's photo and you would receive some fancy stationery to let people know where to look.

What a nonsense, but the germ of a great idea! Here's where the imagination could take off – a really nice place to go. Their website should be much grander – "Hi, welcome to kid's kingdom. Come and see all the kids and their photos. Do you know anyone in here?" Maybe not quite as brash as that, but forming something really special that proud parents would want their child's photo to be placed in for posterity. Who cares about the stationery when we are dealing 'on the Net'? If the people you want to see the photo can access the site, you could e-mail them. If you need 'snail mail' (as posted and delivered mail is becoming known), you could send a photo. Make it special.

Needless to say, I was not impressed. Why waste time and money on something that has not been thought through properly? Maybe that's not marketing, but to me it is all one and the same thing. If it is intuitively right, then it will work and you will know how best to make it happen.

So where will the web go?

We have taken a walk through an evolving technology at an enormous speed, and I can only hope to scratch the surface. (You can guess by now that I am interested in this subject and believe that it will revolutionise business as we know it). The future is an open book, but the story (a bit like a good Agatha Christie) is starting to evolve. We are at the stage where we can start to guess 'who dunnit'. We may be wrong, but the story is beginning to become clearer.

The Internet, as a free system, will become crowded. It is getting that way now. We can see some of these really big 'portals' like Virgin and Freeserve, and they are getting pretty crowded. Also, many of the good domain names are gone. Equally true, many companies who have no wish to compete on a global market, would be quite happy to use the Internet to secure their future. Indeed, while business may be booming, there will come a time when the 'goldrush' starts to subside.

Where do we go from there – who will be the long-term winners and how will the Internet be used?

A major thing that became lost in the rush to 'get on the Net' was that the technology finally puts the power in the communication chain back in the hands of the receiver, not the provider. So the Internet will start to evolve in the way people will prefer to use it. Okay, we have the current boom on e-commerce and the effect on price, but after a while, the newness will start to wane. The evolution will then start to reflect how people want help, not how people want to give it.

So how may it go? I believe that we will start to build communities that become points of common interest. We will start to move more to an industry focus, getting common points of access around industries (for example drugs) and products. Efforts are being made to develop communities that reflect areas – for instance, I am working with a group from Maldon High Street in Essex to recreate in a virtual form the high street environment, using technology to reverse the negative effects of progress on the local commercial community.

An example of how we can use technology creatively could be the simple shop. Why do people buy from a shop? Tradition says we do, but the Internet is changing that. Here is an idea for you all – could you open a shop that merely displays but does not sell? For papers and magazines, the idea would be preposterous, but for some things, not so. Let us explore in our minds a high street where you can walk around and select things, then go home and buy on the Internet, and have the purchases delivered the next day. It starts to remove some of the reasons people give for not shopping in local centres. Creative thought and a number of people and businesses working together could make anything come true.

Other communities could build around supply chains so that we can have clearer channels to market. Groups of suppliers could start to work together, sharing information to supply complete solutions to their clients rather than their separate little bits. And as we build links, we can of course increase our importance in the chain of events (and our dependence on others).

We will build networks and clubs, and from these, who knows what could evolve? Only to say it will be those with the vision that will shape our future society, but that vision does not require huge amounts of cash, only the belief in ideas and ideals.

Enough to say that with this powerful tool to support you, you could start to build some serious market advantage out of this. If you are just starting out, or have bought this book for some inspiration, then certainly the advent of new technology is one that you must not ignore. Do not use the traditional reasons for procrastinating – too old, not enough time, too expensive, don't understand. Get going while the going's good, and make a move. This section is really trying to show you that this whole area is unfolding as we speak. Do not worry about the technology, it really is not a problem – you don't have to worry about how the telephone works to be able to use it.

A final word of advice is not to listen to prophets of doom. Ignore those who say "don't", or "can't" or "wait". They are yesterday's people, and they won't help your business survive into the future. The Internet is just a means of communicating, like the telephone. You can run a business without the telephone. It is difficult, and the telephone is such an integral part of our lives that we don't even notice ourselves using it. The Internet will be like that. You will be able to do business without it, but it will be very difficult.

www.oldkingcole.co.uk
linden@oldkingcole.co.uk

15

Your Action Plan

I do not know you. I only know that, if you are reading this, you (or someone you know) must have bought this book. So, we come full circle, back to chapter 2, and the need for action. If you don't commit to action, all your good intentions will be of no value.

The problem with most people is well-meaning good intentions, and the promise to do something tomorrow. But tomorrow never comes, and next year you will be as you are now, wishing but never doing anything to turn your wishes into reality. We have already discussed this at length, and you know I'm right anyway, don't you!

That would be a shame. If you have read this far, then you will at least be seriously interested in starting your own business or improving the one you already own (because I expect there will be many who read this to see if I can add anything to their ideas). It would be such a loss if all your good intentions came to nought.

> ## What we need is action
> ### - not good intentions

You and I need to ensure that your best intentions turn into reality. The best way to ensure that is that you set up your own 'Start my own Business' or 'Improvements' action plan. This is a simple list of what you will do, and when you will do it. The 'Business Planning' section or information from the banks (and their Business Planning information) will help significantly if, like many, you still need a shove to get you going.

It is not easy to start; I know that and so do you. But the going gets easier as you get further into it. You know that too. You may decide to start in a small way, and hang on to your current job as it suits at the moment. It may mean you start preparing but with the intention of starting properly some time in the future. That is for you to decide, not me. It is not for me to develop your business, not unless you want me as an active partner ... and I don't think you would want that!

PERSONAL ACTION PLAN FOR				
DATE	ACTION NEEDED	BY	DUE DATE	OK?

How to use the action plan

There is no point trying to be anything less that totally open when planning a business. The way to use this action plan is simplicity itself. There is no point in making it complicated. Use it as you want.

- Ideally, the date you decided to do something is the first column, not when you will do it by, but when did you have the idea.

- Next, what is it you're going to do, or if a friend will do it for you, who are they. This just gives a record of who agrees to do a job.

- The due date is the date it will be done by, and this need not be either too aggressive, or too far into the future. A realistic date that everybody can 'buy into'.

- Then tick the last column when it's done (I also like to keep a record of when it was finished, for my own sake).

A trick with using the action plan is to make it a rolling checklist of what you've done, keep a record, and use it as a document to review progress. The process of review is quite simple. Sit down with a spouse, partner or friend, and literally go through action by action. Not to rehash the merit of doing it, more how well are you getting on. If you feel someone will ask you how you're getting on, you will be more focussed in doing it. All the action plan does is makes activity – or lack of it – visible.

Remember also to plan carefully your use of the Internet. That takes as much careful thought as any other type of planning and execution.

Six Honest Serving Men

So the easiest thing to do is start planning and use your action plan, follow the steps in the book to develop your ideas and reasoning. What do you think you want to do, where do you want to do it and when will you have started by, who will you do it with and for, and why should they buy from you. How will you make it all work. Yes, back to basics, back to Kipling's Honest Serving Men.

Who? What? Where? When? Why? How?

The easy way is to be open, talk to others about your ideas, bring things out into the open, even if only with a well-trusted confidant. Do not keep things to yourself, unless you have superhuman determination, in which case it doesn't matter. Make it so that you have to answer to others when they ask how well your plans are going.

But above all you need an action plan. It doesn't need to be fancy, but you do need a list of what you are going to do, by when, so that you can see and evaluate progress – and so can others. It is easier said than done, and it requires discipline. It could be in a book form, it could be on sheets of paper, it could even be on the back of a fag packet or written on the bedroom wall. It doesn't matter.

By developing an action plan, you will consciously or unconsciously have decided a goal and the main steps of how you are going to get there. The rest is down to you – to make happen what you decide to do. Get help, take advice, visit the library, and go see the Enterprise Agency, talk to whoever will add value. Remember too, to avoid those people who are merchants of doom, those that like to inform you of what you can't, rather than can do. Avoid such people like the plague!

When you have made your first million, if you feel that this book added something and gave you a good start, come back and tell me. I would like to know. Perhaps then you can buy me that drink that I've been promising myself all the time I've been sitting here at my word-processor!

Oh and yes, one final thing –

May the Gods go with you!

Appendix

Business Links – Useful contact numbers

Starting off in business can be a very lonely business, and it may be just a bit frightening. There will always be someone to talk to, someone who is sympathetic to what you are trying to do, and is there to help you in your hour of need. The Small Business Service is largely centred on your local Business Link who wants to be your first port of call. If they can help, they will. And if you deserve free access to assistance then they will be able to access it for you.

Business Link (Development Agencies in other areas not named below) is not a centre just for advice, it is a centre for all forms of public help, and a major centre for good quality help from the private sector. Perhaps you will be asked to talk to an Enterprise Agency, or meet with a counsellor, but these people will know you should speak to first. They are the first link in the chain. Listen to what they have to say.

- It may be grant searches you want, or just help in setting up your business.

- It may be business planning or help with computing skills.

- Perhaps you need training, or maybe just advice.

- Maybe all you need is a friendly person to talk to.

- Could it be planning permissions, or advice on health and safety?

- Maybe legal issues, or advice on import or export?

- Could it be design advice or patents?

- Or do you just want general business experience to call upon?

Business Link is ideally placed. These people do not pretend to be experts in any particular area, but they do have access to enormous resources of expertise, and are the prime source for any financial help you may qualify for. You will never know how they may help you until you call.

There are two national reference numbers shown below which will help you to make contact with your local Business Link office. The lists available are always completely up-to-date, so you can be sure of making contact with the best people in your area. These groups are easy to find, so, if you prefer, you can simply pick up a telephone directory, ask at your local council or look in the local business press – most papers run a business section where your local support services advertise – and who carry examples of companies and people they have helped, often people just like you.

As I come to the end of writing this book, I am aware how few folk actually know of the help for people like you. It is there, use it. Only a few weeks ago, a group of students came to my office for an introduction. I was appalled that none had heard of Business Link, and the value they could add. Call them, here is a number to start, and if the number you want isn't here, it is not far away. Go looking.

Contact numbers

☎ **BUSINESS LINK NATIONAL SIGNPOST LINE**

0845 7567765

This point of contact will give you the location and telephone number of the Business Link nearest to your base. From that local centre, you will be able to acquire the names of the people most likely to be able to offer you the precise sort of help that you need for your particular circumstances.

🖥 **BUSINESS LINK NATIONAL WEBSITE**

www.businesslink.co.uk

This point of contact will also give you the relevant details of all local Business Links, as well as other useful information about the services offered.

🖥 **SMALL BUSINESS SERVICE WEBSITE**

www.businessadviceonline.org

This signposting website has information about every aspect of interest to small business, including sources of advice and help and lists of banks, solicitors, accountants and so on. On line since March 2000, this site is seriously comprehensive and of great use to all small businesses, whether established or still in the embryo stage.

INDEX